WHAT OTHERS ARE SAYING

*This is **so needed**, especially for parents who have picked up shame and condemnation and have **lost hope**. God is so faithful to us and He will be to our children also. We are counting on it! Thank you for a beautiful plan for building an army of God-fearing, praying parents. We cannot allow our child's crises of faith to become our crises of faith.*

Cheryl Wells
Side By Side Ministries

Parenting adult children brings a whole new set of challenges. This prayer book does an amazing job of giving some really practical ways for parents to love, encourage and pray for their adult children. And in going through it, it also lifts your eyes to remind YOU of the character and worthiness of our God.

Jon Duey, Pastor
Indianola Community Church

When asked to join the "Your Soul to Keep" prayer group, we didn't know anyone and had a lot of questions. Would confidentiality be kept? Will we be able to open up honestly? What will others think of our family? Now that our group is established, we can say confidently that the friendships we've formed enrich our lives and the lives of our children in ways we didn't think possible.

Rick & Carol
Your Soul to Keep, Group Members

We didn't know all the members of the group so we were apprehensive about sharing concerns about our children, and nervous about praying out loud. It's now a group of people we trust with our greatest concerns and a group we have fun with. If you're trying to decide whether or not this is something to add to your life, do it! The more people praying for our kids the better!

Wanda & Glenn
Your Soul to Keep, Group Members

YOUR SOUL TO KEEP

*A prayer book for praising God as you
pray for your adult kids*

KRISTI DUSENBERY

ISBN: 9798218195694

Scripture quotations, unless otherwise indicated, have been taken from the Christian Standard Bible®, Copyright © 2017 by Holman Bible Publishers. Used by permission. Christian Standard Bible® and CSB® are federally registered trademarks of Holman Bible Publishers.

Printed in the United States of America

The Laughing Grandma
Indianola IA 50125

www.TheLaughingGrandma.com

DEDICATED TO

Our precious army of prayer warriors,

who keep us grounded, encouraged, and well-fed.

We adore you.

And to our kids, who keep our prayer list full

and our hearts fuller. You were born for each other,

so wherever life takes you, stick together.

(Proverbs 17:17)

"The rain fell, the rivers rose, and the winds blew and pounded that house. Yet it didn't collapse, because its foundation was on the rock."

Matthew 7:25

Table of Contents

GETTING STARTED

"You'll never be a perfect parent, but you can

be a praying parent...Your prayers for your children

are the greatest legacy you can leave."

Mark Batterson

Now I lay you at His feet
and pray the Lord your

SOUL TO KEEP

May angels guard you through your life
and guide you in God's perfect light.

These words are my whole-heart's prayer for our adult kids. They fully belong to God. Their souls are fully in His hands. And even though it's been true since the first moment we held them in our arms, letting go of the details of parenting feels unnatural...even undoable at times. The *simple* reality is that our role as their parents changed profoundly the moment they left home...because that's the way it's supposed to be.

Instead of being "children under our authority," they've become fellow adults under God's authority, who need a positive Christian relationship with their parents as they make their own way in the world. It's an important transition that every parent goes through and it often puts a magnifying glass on our regrets, causing us to question the job we did and making us feel less significant somehow. But becoming the parent of adult kids is not a demotion. In many ways, it's more important than ever before; requiring more grit, more emotional stamina, more wisdom, and more dependence on God than we ever imagined.

Several years ago, our need for grit and emotional stamina was shoved into overdrive when we received a phone call from one of our sons. His marriage was in crisis and we never saw it coming. Truth is, the reality of his words nearly broke us. We felt sad, afraid, and angry. We worried about our son, worried about our daughter-in-law, and worried about our grandbabies. Most of all, we were utterly consumed by feelings of helplessness.

All we could do was to love them, speak God's truth...and pray. As humbling as it is to admit, I prayed more for their marriage in those few days than I had in many previous months combined. Nothing kick-starts a prayer life faster than pain, and nothing sends us running into the arms of God quite like the sudden realization that we have absolutely no control over anything.

During that difficult time, *Your Soul to Keep (YSTK)* was born – not the book, but the process. Tim and I needed support from our peers and we needed them to pray, but we realized quickly that it was an awkward leap from casual, *safe* conversation to sharing the painful, ugly details of life. Even though we had wonderful friends who were very glad to pray, we hadn't been purposeful in developing trust and transparency regarding our adult kids. I suppose we were caught up in the social-media mentality of only sharing the good stuff, while keeping the *ugly* tucked neatly away. There was definitely something missing.

As the dust continued to whirl more than settle, we reached out to three couples (also parents of adult children) and invited them to meet with us, to pray specifically for the minds, bodies, and souls of our adult kids. None of us attend the same church and some hadn't even met each other, but we believed this was the direction God was leading. All three couples agreed and the rest, as they say, is history.

Many years later, I find myself ironically grateful for the crisis in our son's marriage; not grateful for the pain, but for the healing. He and his wife are stronger as individuals and as a family because of what they went through, and we are intensely more aware of the importance of prayer...and fellow prayer warriors.

Let me be clear. The habit of praying for our adult kids hasn't become so important because the words we say are so holy or because they've *fixed* every problem. Clearly not. The habit of prayer has become important because it connects us intimately with the God of the universe and we find peace in his presence every time. HE is the one who knows every intimate detail about the minds, bodies, and souls of our adult kids. HE is the one who loves them more than we ever can. And HE is the one who is able to do above and beyond all that we ask or think according to the power that works in us. (Ephesians 3:20)

Our precious YSTK army has praised God from the mountaintops and cried out to him from the valleys: surgeries, broken relationships, pregnancies, sick babies, lost jobs, new jobs, weddings, depression, college graduations, crippling anxiety, miscarriage, substance abuse, promotions, financial hardships, and crises of faith...just to name a few. We laugh. We celebrate. And we cry. We share the burden of waiting for answers that may never come, we encourage each other to consider things from new perspectives, and we are completely vulnerable about our parental fears and failures...without judgment. What a blessing!

This prayer book is the unintended byproduct of our prayer group's journey. And it's the result of much trial and error, as we worked to get ourselves organized. I'm so excited to share it with you and believe passionately that God will use it to bless you as you trust him with the process.

There are two ways to use the resources and organizational tools provided in the following pages. First, they can guide your personal prayer time for your adult kids. Second, they can help you to establish a mighty army of soldiers who will join with you in surrendering your adult kids into the loving arms of their Creator and praying for God's Spirit to move in their lives. The monthly prayers are based entirely on scripture, allowing every member (especially those who may be uncomfortable praying aloud) to confidently claim God's Word on behalf of their adult kids. We are promised that scripture is *"living and effective and sharper than any double-edged sword, penetrating as far as the separation of soul and spirit, joints and marrow. It is able to judge the thoughts and intentions of the heart."* (Hebrews 4:12) What a privilege to have such a powerful weapon at our fingertips, especially in times of crisis.

"True prayer is a way of life,

not just for use in cases of emergency.

Make it a habit, and when the need

arises you will be in practice."

Billy Graham

Seven Reasons to Pray for Our Adult Kids

1-Prayer cultivates a healthy perspective

"For our momentary light affliction is producing for us an absolutely incomparable eternal weight of glory. So we do not focus on what is seen, but on what is unseen. For what is seen is temporary, but what is unseen is eternal." 2 Corinthians 4:17-18

If we believe that God really is who he says he is, and we have faith in the death and resurrection of Jesus, then we have absolute assurance that every problem we face is temporary. It almost never feels like it, but it's always true. And it's a promise we can focus on during dark days.

Since the world began, bad things have been happening that human minds struggle to understand: The Israelites (God's chosen people) suffered in slavery for decades. Paul (one of the most influential leaders in establishing God's church) was beaten and beheaded. Jesus (God's own son) suffered a horrific death on the cross.

Corrie Ten Boom (a passionate Christian who worked with her family to help Jews escape during World War II) was imprisoned, sent to a concentration camp, and narrowly escaped the gas chamber. Beautiful, spunky Maddy (who loved Jesus and was kind to everyone) lost her battle with cancer when she was just twelve years old.

The list of bad things that happen to faith-filled people is long. Clearly, God doesn't promise easy lives and prayer doesn't promise protection from pain. Not in this life.

But.

Prayer *does* invite the Holy Spirit to unleash perspective; perspective that reminds us of the promise that we can survive whatever life throws at us. When we see only scattered pieces, prayer brings confidence that God sees our whole picture and that our struggle has purpose. It isn't forever. Through prayer, we receive the strength to shift our focus away from the ugly, uncertain, gritty pieces of our lives and toward the promise that God will use every piece for good.

2-Prayer is a healthy way to handle anxiety

"Don't worry about anything, but in everything, through prayer and petition with thanksgiving, present your requests to God. And the peace of God, which surpasses all understanding, will guard your hearts and minds in Christ Jesus." Philippians 4:6-7

Let's face it, having adult kids (and grandkids) gives us something to worry about ALL...THE...TIME. We worry about their health, relationships, spiritual condition, finances, careers, how they parent, how they treat others and how they are treated...you name it! Our hearts can get so entangled in a web of worry that we see no way out. But prayer gives us a safe place to speak our fears, to evaluate whether or not our anxious thoughts are reasonable, to accept our need to let go of what we can't control, and to receive supernatural peace. By simply speaking the truth about things that make us anxious, we diminish their power over us. We untangle the web so we can process problems in a healthy way, instead of letting the "yuk" stew in our bellies and brains.

Prayer is a form of therapy that is available every second of every day, without cost. Most of all, it promises comfort for our minds and hope for our hearts when the valleys are deep...especially when they're deep. Jesus was in such anguish before his arrest that "his sweat was like drops of blood falling to the ground." And what did he do? "...he prayed more earnestly..." (Luke 22:44) Moms and Dads, we need no other proof that prayer is a healthy, Biblical way to deal with our anxious thoughts.

3-Prayer unleashes divine power

"...we do not wage war according to the flesh, since the weapons of our warfare are not of the flesh, but are powerful through God for the demolition of strongholds. We demolish arguments *and every proud thing that is raised up against the knowledge of God, and we take every thought captive to obey Christ."* 2 Corinthians 10:3-5

The battles of this life require more of us than we can possibly give. In fact, the one saying you'll never see on a mug in my cupboard is: *God never gives us more than we can handle.* Every parent on the planet knows that we're given more than we can handle every single day. Every. Single. Day.

I'm not one to wrestle with the theology of where trials come from. Maybe God *gives* them to us, maybe he *allows* them, and maybe bad stuff just happens because we live in a really sinful world. Regardless of where trials come from, one thing is certain: God has divine power to fight for us (Exodus 14:14). Prayer unleashes his power to *demolish* strongholds, to *demolish* lies, and to *demolish* the enemy's plans. Moses prayed and the sea split. Joshua prayed and the sun stood still. Daniel prayed and the mouths of the lions stayed shut. Jesus prayed and Lazarus was raised from the dead. When we pray, that same power is alive in us.

4-Prayer leads to better decisions

"Trust in the Lord with all your heart, and do not rely on your own understanding; in all your ways know him, and he will make your paths straight." Proverbs 3:5-6

The process of raising kids teaches us so much. Through the years, we become more disciplined and learn to discipline, we learn to love more deeply, manage stress, mediate conflict, and become masterful multitaskers. The job description of a parent requires it. And if we're not careful, the human skills and abilities we develop can lead to a false sense of security in our own intellectual arsenal. We begin to lean on our own understanding, instead of seeking God to direct our steps. Prayer slows us down. It causes us to think before we act and gives us time to listen for God's direction before we do or say things we'll regret.

The Bible says, *"If any of you lacks wisdom, you should ask God, who gives generously to all without finding fault, and it will be given to you."* (James 1:5) As wisdom increases, so does our ability to discern when to talk and when to be silent...when to act and when to be still...when to rescue and when to let the chips fall.

5-Prayer strengthens our relationship with God

"Draw near to God, and he will draw near to you..." James 4:8

When each of our three sons went through basic military training, I longed for letters that would tell us about their experiences. When our oldest son was rerouted on his way to Afghanistan, to an unknown destination, I longed for just one phone call telling us he was okay. We crave communication from our children; maybe not when they're toddlers, banging on the bathroom door, but when they're grown and far from home, we crave it. God craves it too.

He established prayer as a powerful tool of communication, between himself and the children he loves; a way for us to stay connected and draw near to him. As we share our desires, disappointments, and heartaches with our heavenly Father in prayer, our hearts become more confident in his love, we *feel* that we are not alone, and our faith is increased. Even if all we can do is sit with him in silence, in an attitude of prayer, his Spirit promises to flood our hearts with hope for tomorrow.

6-Prayer grows our relationship with our adult kids

Though we love our children from the moment they enter our lives, there are times when our relationships can become so strained, so shattered that we struggle to even *like* them. Thank you, Jesus, that the gift of prayer keeps our hearts soft and helps our eyes to see our children through *your* perfect eyes. If we are fortunate enough to have strong relationships with our adult kids, we still have adjustments to make as they move out, get married, become parents, start new jobs, lose jobs, experience heartache...the list is long and unpredictable.

One of the best ways to stay connected with our adult kids through changing times is to ask one simple question...often: *How can I pray for you?* A simple text with this question gives them time to think before responding and it assures that we *hear* the request correctly. Sometimes our kids ask for the usual. Sometimes we learn about new opportunities or struggles. Sometimes, they don't respond at all. And that's okay, too. Asking how we can pray for our kids isn't about fishing for juicy details or guilting them into sharing something that they're not ready to share. It's simply a way to show honest interest in their needs and gain a better understanding of how to pray. Bonus? They develop a habit of thinking about prayer also.

7-Jesus made prayer a priority

"Yet Jesus often withdrew to deserted places and prayed." Luke 5:16

Even Jesus, who is fully God, made time to pray. He prayed often. He prayed in solitude, with friends, and in front of large groups. He prayed for himself, for others, and for God's will to be done. He prayed for the children who came to see him and for the disciples he loved. And he prayed for us:

- That we would be filled with joy (John 17:13)
- That we would be protected from evil (John 17:15)
- That we would find purpose in God's truth (John 17:17)
- That we would have unity with others (John 17:23)
- That we would spend eternity in heaven (John 17:24)
- That we would be filled with God's love (John 17:26)
- That we would be forgiven when we cause God pain (Luke 23:34)

Even now, Jesus petitions his Father on our behalf. (Romans 8:34) If we love him, then we will follow his example. 1 John 2:6 says, *"This is how we know we are in him: The one who says he remains in him should walk just as he walked."* So really, what more do we need to know?

Lone Warrior or Mighty Army?

My family loves war movies. In fact, we have several favorites that we tend to watch on repeat. For me, few things are as inspirational as the heart of a warrior. Whether it's William Wallace rounding up his medieval army of Scottish rebels to defeat the English or Desmond Doss running toward the fight to save 75 wounded soldiers during the Battle of Okinawa...the will to fight in the face of adversity is never more personified than in battle.

When parents commit to pray persistently, we make a strategic choice to step onto a spiritual battlefield and plant our flag, to claim God's territory in the lives of our kids. We're not running into battle with swords, but the enemy is waging war. His plan is to destroy our kids, and prayer is our most powerful weapon.

> *Be sober-minded, be alert. Your adversary*
> *the devil is prowling around like a roaring lion,*
> *looking for anyone he can devour.* 1 Peter 5:8

Throughout the Bible, God uses the language of war as a metaphor for the Christian life. We're told to wear armor (Ephesians 6:11) and to endure hardships like a good soldier wanting to please the commanding officer (2 Timothy 2:3-4). We're told that our battle is against the forces of evil (Ephesians 6:12), that God's Word is sharper than any sword (Hebrews 4:12), and that God himself is our most powerful weapon of war (Jeremiah 51:20).

Make no mistake; we *are* at war. We are *real* soldiers with a *real* enemy and the only way to win is to fight with the weapons God provides.

So, how will you use this prayer book as a weapon of war? Here are three options.

1. Fight as a lone warrior, using the materials in solitude to pray for your kids.
2. Gather a mighty army and use the materials to pray together.
3. Jump onto the battle field with gusto and do both!

Pray about it. There isn't a right or wrong way, so ask the Holy Spirit to guide you to the best option for *you*. Whether you choose to use this prayer book as a lone warrior, with a mighty army, or both, the first and most critical step is to accept that there is value in praying for your adult kids and make it a priority. If you're ready to plant your flag, then it's time to make a battle plan. I promise, you won't be sorry. In fact, I believe you're in for one of the greatest blessings of your life!

Praying as a Lone Warrior

Jesus often withdrew to pray...alone. Matthew and Luke wrote that Jesus went up on the mountain by himself and that he prayed there all night long (Matthew 14:23, Luke 6:12). Mark wrote that Jesus got up very early in the morning and went to a deserted place where he prayed by himself (Mark 1:35). Many other times in scripture, Jesus withdrew to be alone with his Father.

Because of his example, we can be confident that it's good to be still in God's presence and to talk to him in solitude about the burdens and joys in our hearts; to be silent and listen for his voice. Everything you need to stay focused on God and thorough in prayer is included in each month's Battle Plans.

Praying with a Mighty Army

God may lead you, as he did us, to start your own *Your Soul to Keep* prayer group, battling for the hearts, minds, and souls of your adult kids with other parents. The idea of sharing the ugly stuff with others can be pretty uncomfortable, but don't let fear prevent you from taking the leap.

Trust me, it took a "rock your world" moment for us to even consider it. Society tells us to show off our Hallmark moments and keep the rest shoved in a closet, safe from gossip and judgment. But that's how the enemy keeps us trapped in anxiety and isolation. On the beautiful contrary, God brings freedom and healing when we open our hearts to others and allow them to pray for us (James 5:16).

Every warrior in every war movie shows evidence of fear; that brief moment when their eyes grow cold. But that's never where great movies end. Great endings are the result of great acts of courage and hard-fought battles. Moms and Dads, this is your defining moment, when you decide whether to charge into battle or walk off the field. If the Holy Spirit leads you to slay your giants like David, standing alone on the battlefield filled with the presence of the God of Israel, then fight hard and with passion. If he leads you to gather a small army like Gideon, fight hard knowing that the Lord will be with you. (1 Samuel 17, Judges 7)

Either way, the monthly Battle Plans in this prayer book will keep you organized and focused. And as you speak your worries and hopes for your adult kids in prayer, with a thankful heart, the peace of God, which surpasses all understanding, will guard your hearts and minds in Christ Jesus. (Philippians 4:6-7)

Understanding the Monthly Battle Plans

Each month, five weapons guide you through the battle: (1) Fellowship, (2) Truth about one of God's names in scripture, (3) Worship songs, (4) Requests & Celebrations charts, and (5) Scripture-based prayers. These weapons are described on the following pages and may be used by lone warriors, mighty armies, or both. Get familiar with the options and then ask God to guide your next steps.

Trust in the Lord with all your heart,
and do not rely on your own understanding;
in all your ways know him, and he will make
your paths straight. Proverbs 3:5-6

Weapon #1: Fellowship

In Acts 2:42-47, Peter describes how the early church practiced fellowship by devoting themselves to one another:

- They learned God's Word.
- They ate together in each other's homes, with glad and sincere hearts.
- They prayed together.
- They were filled with awe at God's miracles.
- They spent time together regularly.
- They had much in common.
- They praised God together.
- They gave to those in need.
- They were used by God to bless others and share in their salvation.

Scripture celebrates the fellowship of these early believers; meeting with your YSTK groups is a beautiful way to follow their example. To learn more about each other and grow deeper connections, Fellowship Starters are provided to kick off each meeting. These questions can be asked as you mingle or once everyone is seated. Lone warriors can simply skip this part of the Battle Plan.

Weapon #2: Devotions About God's Names in Scripture

God's Word is a powerful sword in our hands and readies us for battle (2 Timothy 3:16-17, Ephesians 6:17). What if William Wallace and his army had run into the Battle of Falkirk without swords? What if they failed to prepare for the fight? The Scottish story would have ended much differently. Not only did they use swords to fight, they trained diligently to use them skillfully. In the same way, we must train diligently for life's battles by knowing God's Word and preparing to use it skillfully. Running into battle without it is simply foolish.

Each month, there is a devotion focused on one of God's names from scripture, followed by questions to help you apply his attributes to your life as a parent.

> *Those who know your **name** trust*
> *in you because you have not abandoned*
> *those who seek you, Lord.* Psalm 9:10

Charles Spurgeon wrote, "knowledge is best when it exercises itself upon the Name of God. This most excellent knowledge leads to the most excellent grace of faith. O, to learn more of the attributes and character of God...By knowing His Name is also meant an experimental acquaintance with the attributes of God, which are every one of them anchors to hold the soul from drifting in seasons of peril." (Spurgeon, 1881)

If you choose to start a YSTK group, part of your first meeting will be deciding how to use the devotionals. You may incorporate them into meetings or choose to study them on your own. It's really just a matter of time and preference.

The attributes of God, revealed in his names, are an anchor that keeps us from tossing back and forth on life's crashing waves. And wow, do parents of adult children need an anchor! We need the Lord who provides, who stays with us, who heals, who sanctifies, and fights for us. We need a shepherd. We need the Wonderful Counselor, Mighty God, Eternal Father, and Prince of Peace. We need the Lord who sees every detail of our battle and remains completely in control.

The monthly devotions provide a way to quiet your heart and focus your mind on the goodness and power of God, before calling on him in prayer.

Weapon #3: Worship Songs

Each month, songs are suggested that lead you to worship God according to his name presented in the devotional. It's a way to engage in purposeful praise and recognition of God as our great Commander.

When the army of Edom came to attack the people of Judah, worship was their greatest weapon: "Jehoshaphat appointed some to sing for the Lord and some to praise the splendor of his holiness. When they went out in front of the armed forces, they kept singing: 'Give thanks to the Lord, for his faithful love endures forever.'" The moment they began their shouts and praises, the Lord set an ambush against their enemy, and the army of Judah was victorious. (2 Chronicles 20:21-22)

Judah was outnumbered but still they advanced, praising God for his holiness and splendor, and their enemy was defeated. While our current culture celebrates self-sufficiency and personal victories, we must understand how completely powerless we are without God.

Over and over, scripture shows us why singing is so important.

GOD COMMANDS IT. "*Let the word of Christ dwell richly among you, in all wisdom teaching and admonishing one another through psalms, hymns, and spiritual songs, singing to God with gratitude in your hearts.*" (Colossians 3:16)

Worship songs may be listened to on your own, as a way to prepare your heart for prayer. They may also be used for background music at YSTK meetings or listened to before praying together.

IT'S AN EXPRESSION OF GOD'S SPIRIT IN US. "*I will sing praise with the spirit, and I will also sing praise with my understanding.*" (1 Corinthians 14:15)

When discussing how music is prompted by the Spirit, John MacArthur writes, "The Spirit-filled life produces music. Whether he has a good voice or cannot carry a tune, the Spirit-filled Christian is a singing Christian. Nothing is more indicative of a fulfilled life, a contented soul, and a happy heart than the expression of song." (MacArthur, 2016)

JESUS WORSHIPED IN SONG. "*Jesus is not ashamed to call them brothers and sisters, saying: I will proclaim your name to my brothers and sisters; I will sing hymns to you in the congregation.*" (Hebrews 2:11-12)

GOD HIMSELF SINGS OVER US. "*The Lord your God is among you, a warrior who saves. He will rejoice over you with gladness. He will be quiet in his love. He will delight in you with singing.*" (Zephaniah 3:17)

Bottom line? We need to make time to worship God in song, regardless of when, where, or how.

Weapon #4: Requests and Celebrations

Each month's Battle Plan provides Requests and Celebration charts for each adult child. Though there are boxes for different categories, it's not necessary to fill all of them in for each child. Some months, there may only be one or two things recorded.

This will be the biggest chunk of the monthly YSTK meetings. It's the time for each person to share what has been happening in the lives of their adult kids. Sometimes there is a lot to share and sometimes it's a simple, "same as last month."

It's okay! The point is, it's important to declare what we're thankful for and what we're burdened by, whether it's in writing or spoken aloud, because it keeps unspoken fears from becoming fuel for heartache and worry.

God says, "Don't worry about anything, but in everything, through prayer and petition with thanksgiving, present your requests to God. And the peace of God, which surpasses all understanding, will guard your hearts and minds in Christ Jesus." Philippians 4:6-7

Honor him by recognizing every good thing with a grateful heart and presenting *every* request to him...not just the safe, socially acceptable stuff. *Everything.* We give it all to God and then trust him with it, remembering that our kids' desires, and our desires for them, aren't always what's best. It is only when we surrender those *desires* into the sufficient hands of God that we experience lasting peace. The monthly charts are a perfect tool for brainstorming your "everything."

TIP: If you plan to pray with a mighty army, fill out the grids for your own kids prior to each meeting so you can think through what and how to share. We use one grid per adult child. In other words, one grid for Derek and Hannah, one for Kohl and Bailey, and one for Sam and Skyler...three grids, not six. Make sense? As always, do what works best for you.

Weapon #5: Personal Prayer Coloring Pages

Each month's battle plan includes a coloring page to guide your personal prayer time. If your mind is like mine, it is off to the races as soon as you start to pray. All of the sudden, it's thinking of things to do, things to buy, people to call...you name it! The personal prayer coloring pages are a wonderful tool for keeping us focused. Simply pray for the person or topic in each space as you color the design.

Weapon #6: Scripture-based Prayers

The monthly prayers help us to surrender our kids into the loving, warrior arms of their Creator, asking him to flood their minds, bodies, and souls with his Spirit. It's not about speaking a list of demands or getting desired answers. It's about humbling ourselves to his will and inviting him to be present in the lives of our kids as he works out *his* best plans for them...even when they don't align with our own.

The prayers are based on scripture because that's what God's people did in Nehemiah 9. It's what David did in Psalm 105. It's what the disciples did in Acts 4. And it's what Jesus did in Mark 15.

God's Word is holy and active; using it in our prayers keeps us focused and aligned with Truth. It teaches us to dwell only on things that are true, honorable, just, pure, lovely, commendable, morally excellent, and praiseworthy (Philippians 4:8-9). The only way we can do that is by knowing God's Word and speaking it back to him in prayer.

> **If you feel apprehensive about praying aloud with a YSTK group, I urge you to consider two things. First, God says, "where two or three are gathered together in my name, I am there among them." (Matthew 18:20) Second, YSTK prayers are designed to be read aloud, round-robin style; perfect for those who are not accustomed to praying in front of others.**

"When they arrived, they went to the room upstairs

where they were staying: Peter, John, James, Andrew, Philip,

Thomas, Bartholomew, Matthew, James the son of Alphaeus, Simon

the Zealot, and Judas the son of James. They all were continually

united in prayer, along with the women, including Mary the

mother of Jesus, and his brothers."

Acts 1:13-14

DEPLOY A MIGHTY ARMY

A guide to joining with other parents to pray
for the hearts, souls, and minds of your adult kids

"A wise warrior is better than a strong one,

and a man of knowledge than one of strength;

for you should wage war with sound guidance—

victory comes with many counselors".

Proverbs 24:5-6

Recruit Your Troops

The most important strategy when choosing who to invite to your YSTK prayer group is to seek God's direction. He is the Commander who paired Moses with Aaron, Naomi with Ruth, and Jesus with his disciples. Trust him to lead you to your fellow soldiers. He may surprise you! Whether you are the one inviting others, or you have been invited, ask the Holy Spirit to guide you. Your army may be made up of people from your church, neighborhood, friend-group, workplace, or a mix of these. The priority is that each soldier is committed to these mutual goals:

- To carry one another's burdens (Galatians 6:2)
- To love and support each other through adversity (Proverbs 17:17)
- To provide encouragement and accountability (Proverbs 27:17)
- To invite God's presence (Matthew 18:20)
- To commit to meeting together (Hebrews 10:24-25)
- To assist each other in battle (Ecclesiastes 4:9-12)
- And to pray (Acts 1:14)

When Tim and I began recruiting our troops, we asked God to lead us to the *right* people, and we ended up inviting three couples. Even though we were already acquainted with them, not all of them knew each other so we were definitely asking them to take a risk. Before making a final commitment, we suggested a sort of "blind date" for our first gathering, where we would enjoy a meal, get to know each other, and talk about what our meetings would look like. If any person didn't feel comfortable continuing, we would completely understand. No pressure!

Thankfully, we made a match. All three couples agreed to keep meeting and we now have a beautiful, eclectic group of soldiers from different communities, churches, and even friend groups. The common thread is that each of us wants God's best for our adult kids and each is motivated to pray for guidance.

If you are the one gathering the army, resist the urge to jump into action by inviting obvious choices. Pray first. Ask God to open your eyes to people you may not have considered. We have been so blessed by our fellow soldiers and have established unexpected friendships with people who have grown to love our kids. I can't imagine doing life without them!

At the time we began meeting, two of our three sons were already married and one was engaged. We had three young grandbabies and were still finding our feet with the whole "parenting adults" thing. Though not all of the adult kids we pray for in our group are married or have kids, they are all of a similar age and I believe this commonality has increased our ability to empathize with one another and, quite frankly, to prevent anyone from becoming the resident expert. Trust me, we are all figuring it out together as we look to God's Word for guidance and this (in my opinion) is the best place to be!

You may decide to do this differently. Maybe you will decide to meet with a group of just moms or just dads, instead of couples. Regardless, the most important thing when gathering your troops is to ask the Holy Spirit to lead you every step of the way and to help you develop your strategy. Every group will be as unique as the adult kids they're praying for.

About Your First Meeting

The first time you meet will look quite different from regular monthly meetings because it's all about making a plan. You'll get acquainted, make decisions about what future meetings will look like, and get your group organized. Check out the First Meeting Guide beginning on page 33 for a step-by-step agenda, with resources to get started and keep you on track.

About Monthly Meetings

Ongoing meetings may include any or all of the provided weapons: fellowship starters, devotions, worship songs, updates and celebrations, and scripture-based prayers. The monthly Battle Plans will guide you each step of the way.

Regarding prayer, it took us some time to figure out a plan that we like best, and we still change things up now and then. To prompt discussion, below are a few ways we have organized our prayer time. The key is to be flexible.

- We have read the monthly prayers aloud, round-robin style.
- We have taken turns praying aloud for each child, freestyle or one-sentence for each, and then read the monthly prayers, round-robin style.
- We have taken turns praying personalized prayers for one family of adult kids (focusing on a different family each month) and then read monthly prayers aloud, round-robin style.

Q & A

How many people should I invite?

First, you need to decide if you will be a group of couples, a group of moms, or a group of dads. Next, select no more than four families of adult kids. There are four couples in our group and we pray for 22 adult kids, including spouses. Phew! Any more than this would make it very difficult for two reasons. First, it would take much longer to give adequate family updates. Second, it would make it more difficult to feel connected to each child. Though we haven't even met some of the kids we pray for, they feel like our own in many ways. The short answer? Invite a group that represents three or four families. That could be three or four couples, a group of three moms, or a group of four dads. You get the picture.

How do I invite people?

Make a phone call or have a face-to-face conversation. YSTK groups are personal endeavors so invitations should feel personal as well. It might sound something like this, "We are trying to figure out this whole parenting-adults journey and believe it will be great to meet monthly with a few other couples/moms/dads, to pray for our adult kids together. We have a prayer book to use that includes scripted prayers, based on scripture, and we would love for you to consider joining us."

Have a date in mind when you would like to have a response and consider hosting an informal dinner or dessert night where everyone can get to know each other and check things out before committing.

What if someone isn't comfortable praying out loud?

No worries! Prayers are scripted. The enemy would love to use the fear of praying out loud to prevent us from experiencing the power of praying with others for your adult kids. Each month, you will take turns reading prayers, round-robin style. It's the perfect way to pray God's Word and make sure that the fear of praying in front of others is never an obstacle. Of course, praying off-script is also an option.

How often should we meet?

The prayer book is set up for one meeting each month. Of course, each group will decide what works best. Our group meets monthly, from August through May, and then we pray on our own during the summer. The important thing isn't how often you meet as much as being fully committed to attend scheduled meetings.

Do we have to start in a certain month?

No. Whatever works best for your group is what you should do. The materials are set up with January first, but it's easy to start with any month and simply circle around.

How much time should we plan for each meeting?

This depends on whether you share dinner and/or dessert, or just a bit of brief fellowship before going to battle. For several years, we took turns hosting and providing dinner. This is so fun (and delicious!) but it did make for some late nights. Recently, we've decided to skip the meals and just do dessert so everyone can get home at a more decent hour. I suggest planning a minimum of two hours for your first few meetings and just see how it goes. Keep lines of communication open and stay flexible.

What sorts of requests should we share?

Share anything related to your adult children. Of course, life's concerns and celebrations are not limited to our kids, and other needs will surely come up. Still, it's important to be mindful of your group's purpose so the main focus is your kids. Another important consideration is that trust is essential. For your group to grow and thrive, confidentiality is a must.

If you have other questions, email me at Kristi@TheLaughingGrandma.com

FIRST MEETING GUIDE

"For where two or three

are gathered together in my name,

I am there among them."

Matthew 18:20

What to Bring to Your First Meeting

- One YSTK prayer book for each person
- Something to write with
- Reading glasses (ugh!)
- Photos of your kids/family for each member of the group
- Tape or a glue stick
- Open hearts and minds, willing to fully engage

Agenda

- Break the ice
- Decide on a meeting strategy
- Plan upcoming schedule
- Exchange contact information
- Meet the families

Break the Ice

Whether you are brand new to each other or old friends, it's important to be purposeful about growing a positive group dynamic from the start. The questions below will help to kick things off in a fun and non-threatening way. Simply choose a few questions for everyone to answer, have each person choose their own, or write them on pieces of paper and take turns drawing one out of a jar.

- Would you rather give up eating sweets or eating fast food?

- Would you rather have a conversation with the birth mother of Moses or his Egyptian mother?

- Would you rather have unlimited gift cards to one restaurant or one clothing store?

- Would you rather be a "fly on the wall" to hear Moses talking to Pharaoh about the Israelites or Judas talking to the priests about Jesus?

- Would you rather travel the world for a year, all expenses paid, or have $40,000 to spend on whatever you want?

- Would you rather time-travel to talk with your great-great grandparents or your great-great grandkids?

35

- Would you rather watch God create the universe, animals, or humans?

- Would you rather walk on water with Jesus or walk through the Red Sea with Moses?

- Would you rather have to cook the Thanksgiving meal every year or clean it up every year?

- Would you rather have had Jesus as your son or your friend?

- Would you rather live on canned food or ramen noodles?

- Would you rather watch Moses read the 10 commandments or be in the crowd to hear John the Baptist.

- Would you rather have to walk two miles during a cold weather advisory or a hot weather advisory?

- Would you rather have a conversation with Noah about the ark or with Jonah about the whale?

- Would you rather explore a sunken ship or an Egyptian tomb?

- Would you rather be present at the birth of Jesus or his resurrection?

- Would you rather vacation at state parks or in big cities?

- Would you rather wander in the wilderness with Moses or John the Baptist?

- Would you rather witness the worlds beginning or its end?

- Would you rather be a shepherd in Bethlehem or a fisherman on the Red Sea?

- Would you rather meet a famous chef, quarterback, or movie star?

- Would you rather live through a plague of flies or frogs?

- Would you rather be a rodeo clown or the bull rider?

- Would you rather be thrown into a fiery furnace, a lions' den, or the belly of a whale?

- Would you rather only watch war movies or romantic comedies for the rest of your life?

Group Strategy

Use the questions below to decide on a strategy for your monthly meetings. If we have learned anything, it's to be flexible, so allow your strategy to evolve over time. To get started, make on a clear plan so everyone knows what to expect. We've also learned that it's important to discuss personal preferences. Do we need a specific end time or are we okay with leaving it open? Do we want to offer adult beverages or stick with water and coffee? Does anyone have food allergies?

The following chart is designed to guide your discussion and record decisions.

ITEM	NOTES
WHERE *Will we take turns hosting or meet at the same place?*	
WHEN *What days and times work best?*	
FOOD & DRINK *Will we have food/drinks? What kind? Any allergies?*	
AGENDA *Will we use songs and/or devotions during meetings? If so, how?*	
PRAYER *What prayer option do we want to start with? (see bottom of page 30)*	

"They devoted themselves to meeting together and broke bread from house to house. They ate their food with joyful and sincere hearts."

Proverbs 16:3

Meeting Schedule

This chart is place to record when and where you will meet each month. Meetings can begin any month, so just start where you are and circle around.

	DATE	TIME	LOCATION / HOST
JANUARY			
FEBRUARY			
MARCH			
APRIL			
MAY			
JUNE			
JULY			
AUGUST			
SEPTEMBER			
OCTOBER			
NOVEMBER			
DECEMBER			

"Every experience God gives us,

every person He puts in our lives

is the perfect preparation for

the future that only He can see."

Corrie Ten Boom

Contact Information

Use this page to collect contact information for your fellow soldiers. If you prefer, type contact information on a document, print, and attach below.

Member/couple: _____

    Phone number(s): _____

    Email: _____

    Address: _____

Member/couple: _____

    Phone number(s): _____

    Email: _____

    Address: _____

Member/couple: _____

    Phone number(s): _____

    Email: _____

    Address: _____

Member/couple: _____

    Phone number(s): _____

    Email: _____

    Address: _____

"My bones were not hidden from you when I was made in secret...all my days were written in your book and planned before a single one of them began."

Psalm 139:15-16

Meet the Families

For this meeting, focus on getting to know each other's families. The following pages provide a place to record information about the adult kids you will be praying for. You will also notice designated areas for photos. Our group found it very helpful to share photos of each child/family, as a way to connect names with faces. Bring photos of your kids for each member of the group and tape or glue them into the prayer book as each family shares. We simply printed them on plain paper, using a black and white printer. Easy-peasy!

The sample below is about a fictional family, but it shows what the notes pages may look like. This is also a good time to comment on the importance of confidentiality. What's shared with the group, stays with the group.

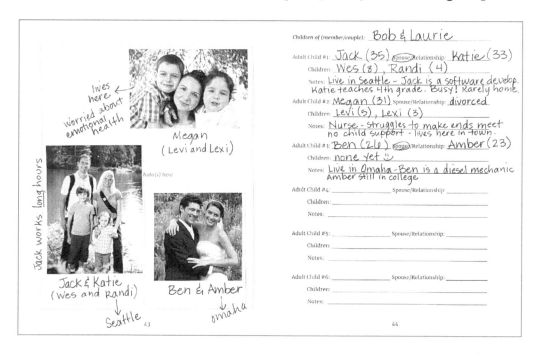

IMPORTANT NOTE ABOUT SHARING: Displaying the grace of Jesus is essential for growing trust and staying authentic. Otherwise, it's a waste of time. So many parents are hurting over their kids' relationship choices, substance abuse, mental health issues, crime, suicide...the list goes on. Our *Lord Who Sees* knows every detail and continues to love unconditionally; not because he agrees with every choice, but because he is compassionate. If our perfect Father can offer grace, then shouldn't we as well? The whole purpose of your YSTK group is to grow a supportive army of soldiers who love each other no matter what, and pray fervently for God to hold the souls of your kids in the palm of his hand.

attach photo(s) here

Adult kids of: _____

Adult Child #1: _____ Spouse/Relationship: _____

    Children: _____

    Notes: _____

Adult Child #2: _____ Spouse/Relationship: _____

    Children: _____

    Notes: _____

Adult Child #3: _____ Spouse/Relationship: _____

    Children: _____

    Notes: _____

Adult Child #4: _____ Spouse/Relationship: _____

    Children: _____

    Notes: _____

Adult Child #5: _____ Spouse/Relationship: _____

    Children: _____

    Notes: _____

Adult Child #6: _____ Spouse/Relationship: _____

    Children: _____

    Notes: _____

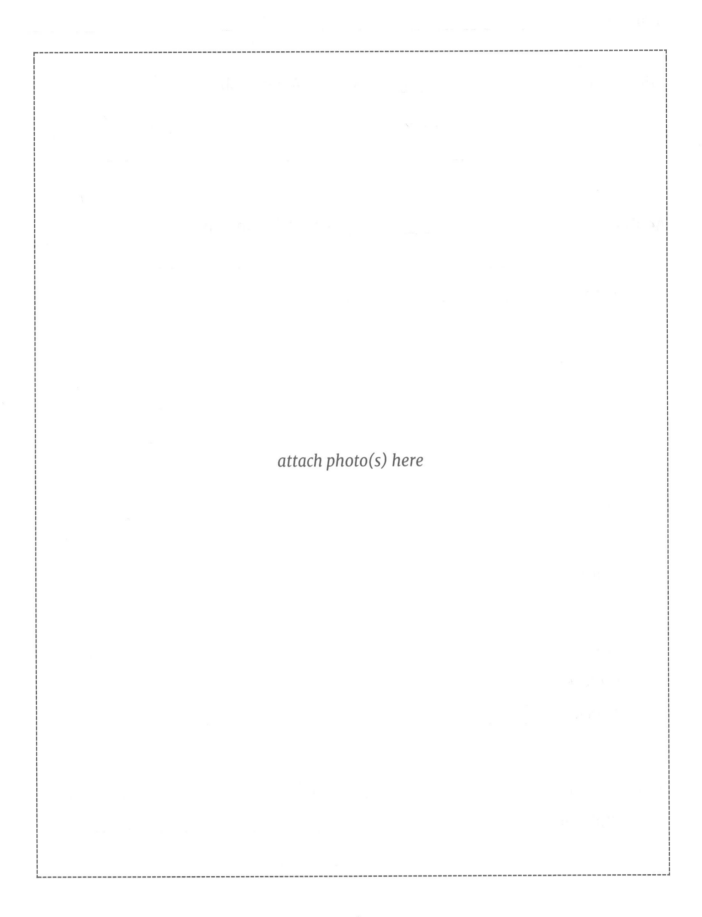

attach photo(s) here

Adult kids of: _____

Adult Child #1: _____ Spouse/Relationship: _____

    Children: _____

    Notes: _____

Adult Child #2: _____ Spouse/Relationship: _____

    Children: _____

    Notes: _____

Adult Child #3: _____ Spouse/Relationship: _____

    Children: _____

    Notes: _____

Adult Child #4: _____ Spouse/Relationship: _____

    Children: _____

    Notes: _____

Adult Child #5: _____ Spouse/Relationship: _____

    Children: _____

    Notes: _____

Adult Child #6: _____ Spouse/Relationship: _____

    Children: _____

    Notes: _____

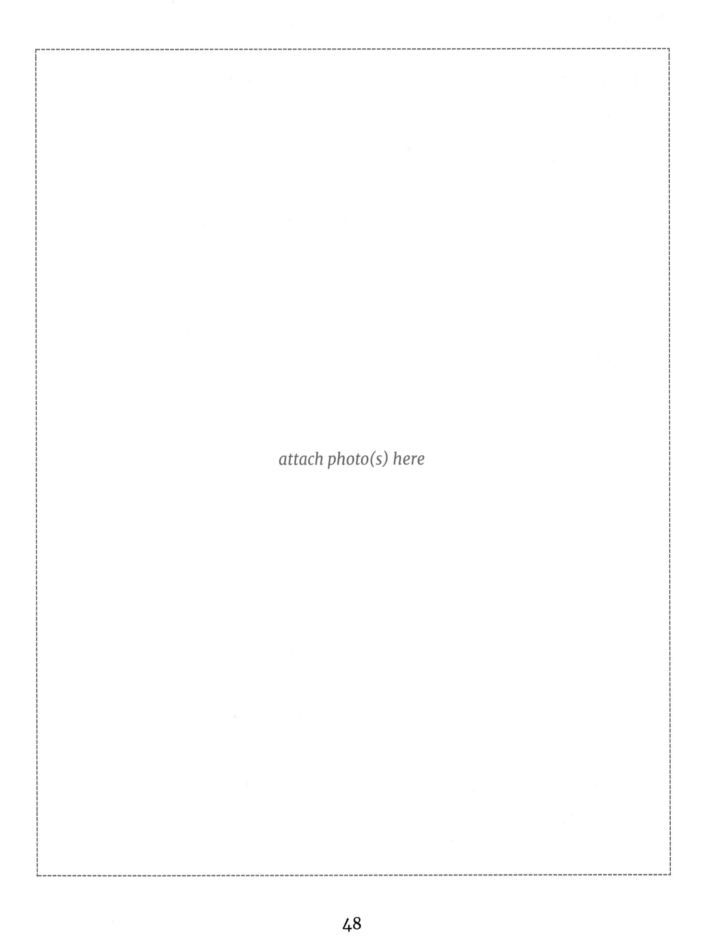

attach photo(s) here

Adult kids of: _____

Adult Child #1: _____ Spouse/Relationship: _____

    Children: _____

    Notes: _____

Adult Child #2: _____ Spouse/Relationship: _____

    Children: _____

    Notes: _____

Adult Child #3: _____ Spouse/Relationship: _____

    Children: _____

    Notes: _____

Adult Child #4: _____ Spouse/Relationship: _____

    Children: _____

    Notes: _____

Adult Child #5: _____ Spouse/Relationship: _____

    Children: _____

    Notes: _____

Adult Child #6: _____ Spouse/Relationship: _____

    Children: _____

    Notes: _____

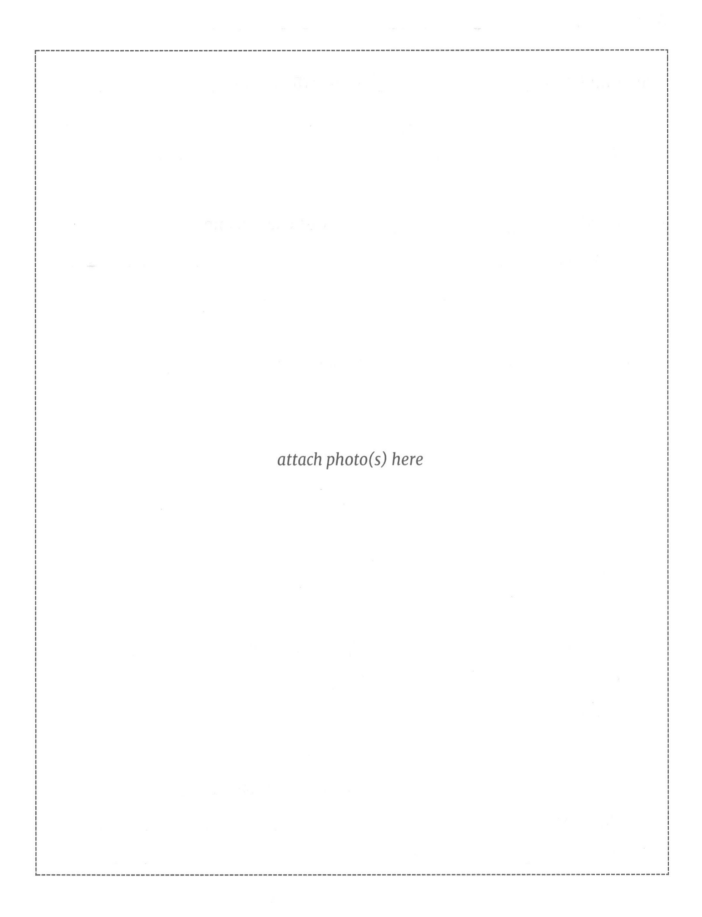

attach photo(s) here

Adult kids of: _____

Adult Child #1: _____ Spouse/Relationship: _____

    Children: _____

    Notes: _____

Adult Child #2: _____ Spouse/Relationship: _____

    Children: _____

    Notes: _____

Adult Child #3: _____ Spouse/Relationship: _____

    Children: _____

    Notes: _____

Adult Child #4: _____ Spouse/Relationship: _____

    Children: _____

    Notes: _____

Adult Child #5: _____ Spouse/Relationship: _____

    Children: _____

    Notes: _____

Adult Child #6: _____ Spouse/Relationship: _____

    Children: _____

    Notes: _____

"Letting go of our 'dependence on independence' and letting someone else take control goes against natural human instinct. We need to fight the urge to take over and just let God be God, because He can provide for us better than we can."

Corallie Thornton

JANUARY BATTLE PLAN

Focus on Jehovah Jireh: The Lord Who Provides

"And Abraham named that place

The Lord Will Provide, so today it is said,

"It will be provided on the Lord's Mountain."

Genesis 22:9-14

January Agenda

- Fellowship
- Focus on Jehovah Jireh: The Lord Who Provides
- Worship
- Requests & Celebrations
- Prayer

Fellowship Starters

The host can ask these questions while mingling or once everyone is seated:

- What's your first choice in a box of assorted chocolates?

- Have you ever binge-watched an entire season of a show in a few days?

Focus on Jehovah Jireh: The Lord Who Provides

This name of God is only used one time in the Bible and it comes just after God tests Abraham's obedience by telling him to sacrifice his only son, Isaac, on an altar of fire. This is Abraham and Sarah's only son. The son they prayed for...ached for...and waited fifty years for.

It's easy to slip into *Sunday school mode* when reading stories from the Bible that have become overly familiar. I don't know about you, but I've heard this story about Abraham several times and it usually congers images of a Hollywood production, ending with Abraham at the altar with a glowing ring of faithfulness around his head. Please understand, I'm not making light of it. Quite the opposite, in fact.

There is nothing *nice* or entertaining about this event. It really happened in human history, and it's horrific.

> *When they arrived at the place that God had told him about, Abraham built the altar there and arranged the wood. He bound his son Isaac and placed him on the altar on top of the wood. Then Abraham reached out and took the knife to slaughter his son.* (Genesis 22:9-10)

It's impossible to imagine the pain and confusion that raged in Abraham's head as he held the knife and looked into the face of his son – the son he dearly loved and was promised as the start of many nations. It's unthinkable. And to be perfectly honest, I question how any parent could even pick the knife up in the first place.

*But the angel of the Lord called to him from heaven and said, "Abraham, Abraham!...Do not lay a hand on the boy or do anything to him. For now I know that you fear God, since you have not withheld your only son from me." Abraham looked up and saw a ram caught in the thicket by its horns. So Abraham went and took the ram and offered it as a burnt offering in place of his son. And Abraham named that place **The Lord Will Provide**."* Genesis 22:9-14

What unfathomable faith. Abraham withheld nothing from God, and God rewarded his obedience by sparing Isaac and providing an alternative sacrifice. See, God knew what Abraham didn't. He saw what Abraham couldn't. And I believe that he empowered Abraham to do what seemed impossible because of his faith that God's Word is trustworthy, and his provision is perfect.

What (or who) are we withholding from God because we aren't fully trusting Jehovah Jireh...the God who provides? It's time to build our fire. It's time to lay our greatest fears and most precious blessings on the altar, and trust that God is quietly working in ways we cannot see, arranging the details of our lives so that we will receive exactly what we need, exactly when we need it.

Making it Personal

What *thing* about my adult children am I holding too tightly?

_____

_____

_____

What provisions am I waiting for in the lives of my adult kids?

_____

_____

_____

Right now, I lay these things on a proverbial altar and surrender them to Jehovah Jireh. (Write your prayer to God on the lines below and ask him to give you the faith you need to trust his perfect provision.)

_____

_____

_____

_____

_____

Worship Songs About Our God Who Provides

The following songs may be used to worship God as you prepare your heart to pray. An easy way to find them is to search "Your Soul to Keep Playlist" on Spotify, where the lyrics will scroll for most songs as you listen. If you are going through an especially difficult time, see the "Songs for Extra Hard Days" list on page 301.

- Blessed Be Your Name | Matt Redman
- Good, Good Father | Chris Tomlin
- Goodness of God | Bethel Music, Jenn Johnson
- Great Are You Lord | Casting Crowns

- _____

- _____

January Requests & Celebrations

The following pages are a place to record prayer requests and celebrations for each adult child. Remember, no need to fill every box. Simply share as desired.

As you color each space, use it as a guide to direct your prayers.

It's time to build our fire. It's time to lay our greatest fears and most precious blessings on the altar, and trust that God is quietly working behind the scenes, arranging the details of our lives so that we will receive exactly what we need, exactly when we need it.

–Your Soul To Keep–

LIVE WITH PURPOSE

PRAISE JEHOVAH JIREH

FRIENDS & NEIGHBORS

PASTORS & MISSIONARIES

HEALTHY RELATIONSHIPS

FINANCIAL PEACE

DESIRE FOR GOD

OUR NATION

GRANDKIDS

GENTLENESS

PHYSICAL HEALTH

NONBELIEVERS

PROTECTION FROM EVIL

WISDOM FOR PARENTING

NEIGHBORS

EXTENDED FAMILY

JOY & CONTENTMENT

PATIENCE

EMOTIONAL HEALTH

KIDS

EXPERIENCE GOD'S POWER

DISCERNMENT

LIVE WITH HOPE

January Requests & Celebrations for: _____

Consider: Celebrations, Mind, Body, Soul, Career & Finances, Family, Relationships

January Requests & Celebrations for: _____

Consider: Celebrations, Mind, Body, Soul, Career & Finances, Family, Relationships

January Requests & Celebrations for: _____

Consider: Celebrations, Mind, Body, Soul, Career & Finances, Family, Relationships

January Requests & Celebrations for: _____

Consider: Celebrations, Mind, Body, Soul, Career & Finances, Family, Relationships

January Requests & Celebrations for: _____

Consider: Celebrations, Mind, Body, Soul, Career & Finances, Family, Relationships

January Requests & Celebrations for: _____

Consider: Celebrations, Mind, Body, Soul, Career & Finances, Family, Relationships

January Requests & Celebrations for: _____

Consider: Celebrations, Mind, Body, Soul, Career & Finances, Family, Relationships

January Requests & Celebrations for: _____

Consider: Celebrations, Mind, Body, Soul, Career & Finances, Family, Relationships

January Requests & Celebrations for: _____

Consider: Celebrations, Mind, Body, Soul, Career & Finances, Family, Relationships

January Requests & Celebrations for: _____

Consider: Celebrations, Mind, Body, Soul, Career & Finances, Family, Relationships

January Requests & Celebrations for: _____

Consider: Celebrations, Mind, Body, Soul, Career & Finances, Family, Relationships

January Requests & Celebrations for: _____

Consider: Celebrations, Mind, Body, Soul, Career & Finances, Family, Relationships

January Requests & Celebrations for: _____

Consider: Celebrations, Mind, Body, Soul, Career & Finances, Family, Relationships

January Requests & Celebrations for: _____

Consider: Celebrations, Mind, Body, Soul, Career & Finances, Family, Relationships

January Requests & Celebrations for: _____

Consider: Celebrations, Mind, Body, Soul, Career & Finances, Family, Relationships

January Requests & Celebrations for: _____

Consider: Celebrations, Mind, Body, Soul, Career & Finances, Family, Relationships

January Requests & Celebrations for: _____

Consider: Celebrations, Mind, Body, Soul, Career & Finances, Family, Relationships

January Requests & Celebrations for: _____

Consider: Celebrations, Mind, Body, Soul, Career & Finances, Family, Relationships

January Requests & Celebrations for: _____

Consider: Celebrations, Mind, Body, Soul, Career & Finances, Family, Relationships

January Requests & Celebrations for: _____

Consider: Celebrations, Mind, Body, Soul, Career & Finances, Family, Relationships

January Prayers

Praising the God Who Provides

We praise you, our Lord who provides peace and grace through Jesus. Your forgiveness is perfect, leading to abundant and eternal life. We can trust you in days of trouble because we know that you will provide endurance, character, and hope that never disappoints. The birds don't sow or reap, yet you provide food and shelter. The wildflowers don't labor or spin, yet you cloth them more beautifully than Solomon in all his splendor. The eyes of all living things look to you and you give them food at the proper time. We are much more valuable to you than these. We will not worry about the details of life because we trust that you already know what we need. As we seek you with all our hearts, you will provide. (Romans 5, Luke 12:24, Psalm 145:15, Matthew 6:25-34)

Experience God's Power

As the new year starts, we know our adult kids will face challenges, just as the disciples faced challenges. When the disciples were in the boat with Jesus, a storm came on them suddenly and ferociously...and they ran to you for strength. May our kids also run to you for help when they are scared and face hard times. When their faith is weak and they become overwhelmed by fear or anxiety, be gracious to them and hear their cries. Rebuke the waves and winds that threaten to overtake them, and show them your power....the kind that brings peace in the midst of chaos. And may it cause them to draw closer to you on stormy nights and sunny days. Regardless of what the year brings, may they see your power in their lives and learn to trust you more. (Matthew 8:23–27)

Protection from Evil

Lord, protect our adult kids from anything that wages war against their souls. Open their eyes to sinful desires that threaten to destroy them and give them the wisdom to run from every evil temptation. We pray that they will run to you for wisdom and love and peace, so they will have pure hearts that lead to an abundant and fulfilled life. Destroy the plans of anyone who tries to lead our kids away from you, and stop any evil plans against them. Crush thoughts of sexual immorality, deception, envy, arrogance, foolishness, greed...and every desire to do evil to others. Instead, may the hearts and minds of our kids be so full of your light and truth that they cannot be spoiled by any destructive thought. (1 Peter 2:11, 2 Timothy 2:22, Mark 23:10-23)

Desire to Know God

Lord, by the power of your Spirit, fill our adult kids with the knowledge that you know everything that's in their hearts - the good, the bad, and the ugly - and that you still love them more than they can possibly imagine. You know every thought they think and every word before they speak it. May this knowledge cause them to desire you more than ever before; to experience your love and to find comfort in your grace. Though we want them to enjoy life, we also pray that they won't desire anything on earth more than they desire you. When they speak to you, fill them with faith that you hear them so they will talk to you about every detail of their lives. If they don't want to speak to you, send your Spirit to change their mind. Be their friend, Jesus...a friend who they will trust to love them, listen to them, and guide them every day. (Psalm 139:1-4, Psalm 73:25, 1 John 5:14-15)

Healthy Relationships

Lord, you created our adult kids to need healthy relationships. Please lead them to friends and soulmates who will make them feel valued and encourage them to make healthy decisions that honor you. Wherever they go - in school, workplace, church, or community - guide our kids to connect with people who love you and cause them to walk away from people who are harmful. We pray for our kids to have marriage relationships that are full of laughter, love, and grace, so they will love each other passionately, faithfully, and unconditionally. Teach our adult kids to bless others, to be a light in this dark world, and to spread the sweet knowledge of you everywhere they go. (Genesis 2:18, Proverbs 13:20, 2 Corinthians 2:14)

Wisdom for Parenting

Perfect Father, teach our adult kids to make you the King of their homes. May they follow the same instructions you gave the Israelites; to love you with all their heart, all their soul, and all their strength...and to teach their kids to do the same. We pray that their homes will be a sanctuary, showing our grandkids the reward of loving you. Open the eyes of our kids to see the value of disciplining their kids with wisdom and grace, so they will raise children who act with restraint and treat others with love and respect. Finally, wherever the enemy causes busyness to threaten the hearts and homes of our kids and grandkids, send your Holy Spirit to convict them so they will see the importance of building time into their days to simply be still as a family. (Deuteronomy 6:4-9, Proverbs 22:15, Hebrews 12:6)

Live with Hope and Purpose

Jesus, fill the hearts of our kids with new hope as they walk into the new year. Cause their eyes to focus on you, so they will never be shaken by uncertainty and give them the wisdom to see new opportunities through the lens of your Truth so they will be protected from walking down wrong paths. When they are on a wrong path, wake them up so they will have the wisdom and courage to change course. You are able to make their best path known to them, so we ask for you to do that in a powerful way. Thank you for creating them with a good purpose. Please give them fresh revelation about your purpose for them so they will be filled with joy and peace, overflowing with hope by the power of your Spirit as they live out their purpose with bold conviction. (Ephesians 2:10, Romans 15:13)

Emotional and Physical Health

Jesus, we believe that you are able to heal the minds, bodies, and souls of our adult kids completely, so we ask for healing. When they don't believe in your power to heal, we pray that your Spirit will invade their hearts and minds, and make your power known to them. Where their minds are broken from hardships, send your healing power to refresh them. Free them from anything that holds them captive to fear or depression and keeps them from enjoying a full and joyful life. When Job lost every single thing in his life - his family, his possessions, and his health - he never stopped talking to you. He never stopped trying to understand your plan for him, and everything he lost was eventually restored. We pray that our kids will do the same thing and that you will restore anything that they've lost. Help us to be patient, God, as we trust your purpose and timing for the healing of our kids. (Jeremiah 17:14, James 5:10-11)

Now to him who is able to do immeasurably more than all we ask or imagine, according to his power that is at work within us, to him be glory in the church and in Christ Jesus throughout all generations, for ever and ever! Amen. (Ephesians 3:20-21)

"The most holy and important practice in the spiritual life is the presence of God – that is, every moment to take great pleasure that God is with you."

Brother Lawrence

FEBRUARY BATTLE PLAN

Focus on Jehovah Shammah: The Lord is There

"My dwelling place will be with them;

I will be their God, and they will be my people."

Psalm 34:3

February Agenda

- Fellowship
- Focus on Jehovah Shammah: The Lord is There
- Worship
- Requests & Celebrations
- Prayer

Fellowship Starters

The host can ask these questions while mingling or once everyone is seated:

- What was your first vehicle?

- On a scale where one is a minimalist and five is a hoarder, where would you rank yourself?

Focus on Jehovah Shammah: The Lord is There

The book of Ezekiel tells the ongoing story of the Israelites' rebellion against God. Fed up, God choose to show the prophet Ezekiel a vision of his plan to unleash judgment on this ungrateful, disobedient people...including banishing them from Jerusalem and even from his own presence. Overwhelmed by what he saw, Ezekiel fell on his face and cried out to God: Is there any hope left? (Ezekiel 11:13)

Seeing Ezekiel's distress, God assures him that the purpose of his judgement is to lead the Israelites to restoration.

> *I will give them integrity of heart and put a new spirit within them; I will remove their heart of stone from their bodies and give them a heart of flesh, so that they will follow my statutes, keep my ordinances, and practice them. They will be my people, and I will be their God. Ezekiel 11:19-20*

One day, he would gather them together again, in a new city with a new temple and a new name. They would have blessings like never before and God's presence would be near them again: "...the name of the city from that time on will be: THE LORD IS THERE (Jehovah Shammah)." Ezekiel 48:35

But even in this new and beautiful city, God's presence would not dwell in their hearts. Instead, it would stay in the tabernacle, where only the priests could enter and only one day each year

Thanks to Jesus, God's presence is no longer confined to a room of marble and stone. Because of Jesus, sin no longer separates us from God. Because of Jesus, God's presence dwells in human hearts. In 1 Corinthians 3:16, Paul writes:

*Don't you yourselves know
that you are God's temple and that
the Spirit of God lives in you?*

If we believe in the death and resurrection of Jesus and receive his gift of salvation, then he is always with us. *He is There*; in every battle, every celebration, and every ordinary moment. Today, we claim the promise that "the tabernacle of God is with men, and He will dwell with them, and they shall be His people. God Himself will be with them and be their God." (Revelation 21:3)

If you aren't sure whether or not God dwells in your heart, go to page 295 to learn how you can be confident in his love, grace, and eternal presence.

Making it Personal

Am I confident that God's presence resides in my heart? If so, how should this change the way I respond to life's challenges?

_____

_____

_____

Am I confident that God's presence resides in the hearts of my adult children? Whether yes or no, how can I remind them of this beautiful truth this week?

_____

_____

_____

On the lines below, write a prayer thanking God for Jesus and asking him to make his presence powerfully known to your kids in specific ways this week.

_____

_____

_____

_____

_____

Worship Songs About the Lord Who Is with Us

The following songs may be used to worship God as you prepare your heart to pray. An easy way to find them is to search "Your Soul to Keep Playlist" on Spotify, where the lyrics will scroll for most songs as you listen. If you are going through an especially difficult time, see the "Songs for Extra Hard Days" list on page 301.

- Another in the Fire (acoustic) | Hillsong UNITED
- Holy Spirit | Francesca Battistelli
- I Am Not Alone | Kari Jobe
- Never Once | Matt Redman
- There Was Jesus | Zach Williams, Dolly Parton

- _____

- _____

February Requests & Celebrations

Use the following pages to record prayer requests and celebrations for each adult child. Remember, no need to fill every box. Simply share as desired.

As you color each space, use it as a guide to direct your prayers.

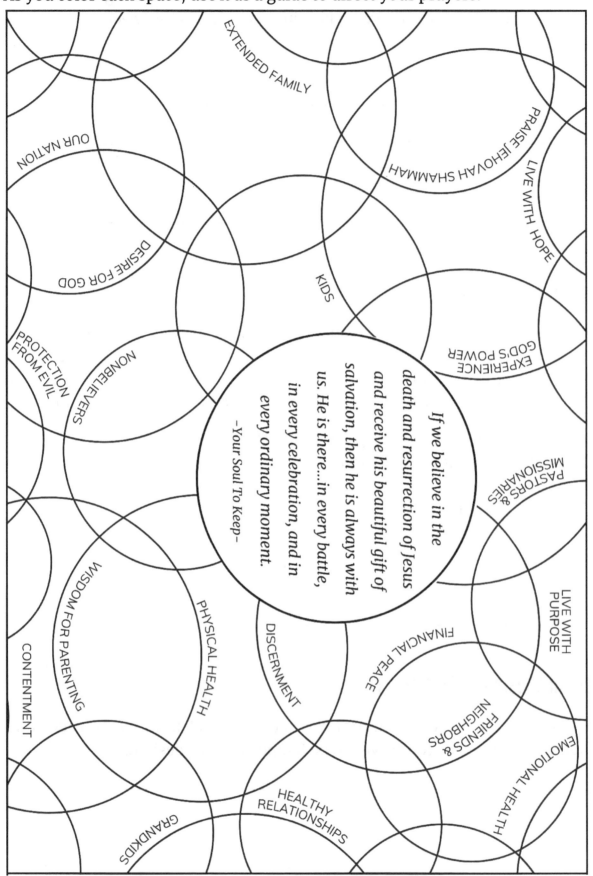

EXTENDED FAMILY

PRAISE JEHOVAH SHAMMAH

LIVE WITH HOPE

OUR NATION

DESIRE FOR GOD

KIDS

EXPERIENCE GOD'S POWER

PROTECTION FROM EVIL

NONBELIEVERS

If we believe in the death and resurrection of Jesus and receive his beautiful gift of salvation, then he is always with us. He is there...in every celebration, and in every ordinary moment.

–Your Soul To Keep–

PASTORS & MISSIONARIES

WISDOM FOR PARENTING

PHYSICAL HEALTH

DISCERNMENT

FINANCIAL PEACE

LIVE WITH PURPOSE

CONTENTMENT

FRIENDS & NEIGHBORS

EMOTIONAL HEALTH

GRANDKIDS

HEALTHY RELATIONSHIPS

February Requests & Celebrations for: _____

Consider: Celebrations, Mind, Body, Soul, Career & Finances, Family, Relationships

February Requests & Celebrations for: _____

Consider: Celebrations, Mind, Body, Soul, Career & Finances, Family, Relationships

February Requests & Celebrations for: _____

Consider: Celebrations, Mind, Body, Soul, Career & Finances, Family, Relationships

January Requests & Celebrations for: _____

Consider: Celebrations, Mind, Body, Soul, Career & Finances, Family, Relationships

February Requests & Celebrations for: _____

Consider: Celebrations, Mind, Body, Soul, Career & Finances, Family, Relationships

February Requests & Celebrations for: _____

Consider: Celebrations, Mind, Body, Soul, Career & Finances, Family, Relationships

February Requests & Celebrations for: _____

Consider: Celebrations, Mind, Body, Soul, Career & Finances, Family, Relationships

February Requests & Celebrations for: _____

Consider: Celebrations, Mind, Body, Soul, Career & Finances, Family, Relationships

February Requests & Celebrations for: _____

Consider: Celebrations, Mind, Body, Soul, Career & Finances, Family, Relationships

February Requests & Celebrations for: _____

Consider: Celebrations, Mind, Body, Soul, Career & Finances, Family, Relationships

February Requests & Celebrations for: _____

Consider: Celebrations, Mind, Body, Soul, Career & Finances, Family, Relationships

February Requests & Celebrations for: _____

Consider: Celebrations, Mind, Body, Soul, Career & Finances, Family, Relationships

February Requests & Celebrations for: _____

Consider: Celebrations, Mind, Body, Soul, Career & Finances, Family, Relationships

February Requests & Celebrations for: _____

Consider: Celebrations, Mind, Body, Soul, Career & Finances, Family, Relationships

February Requests & Celebrations for: _____

Consider: Celebrations, Mind, Body, Soul, Career & Finances, Family, Relationships

February Requests & Celebrations for: _____

Consider: Celebrations, Mind, Body, Soul, Career & Finances, Family, Relationships

February Requests & Celebrations for: _____

Consider: Celebrations, Mind, Body, Soul, Career & Finances, Family, Relationships

February Requests & Celebrations for: _____

Consider: Celebrations, Mind, Body, Soul, Career & Finances, Family, Relationships

February Requests & Celebrations for: _____

Consider: Celebrations, Mind, Body, Soul, Career & Finances, Family, Relationships

February Requests & Celebrations for: _____

Consider: Celebrations, Mind, Body, Soul, Career & Finances, Family, Relationships

February Prayers

Praising the God Who Is with Us

Lord, you search our hearts and know us completely. You know when we sit and when we get up, and you understand our thoughts. You are with us wherever we go, and before we speak a word, you already know it completely. You go before us and behind us, something too wonderful for our minds to understand. We cannot flee from your Spirit. We cannot flee from your presence. If we go to the heavens, you are there. If we go to the grave, you are there. Even if we fly to where the sun rises and sets, your hand will guide and support us. When everything becomes dark around us, your light will shine like the day and you will be near. You have been with us since the day that you knit us together and every moment of our lives are already in your book. (Psalm 139)

Experience God's Power

Dear God, we boldly ask you to send your power into the lives of our adult kids. As Joshua wandered the wilderness with the Israelites, they thought they were blocked by the Jordan river because it was raging at flood stage. Crossing to the other side seemed impossible, but you commanded them to step into the water anyway and to trust you with their destination. As soon as their feet touched the water, your power stopped it so they could cross on dry ground. And this is how they knew that the living God was among them. Pour this kind of faith into the hearts of our adult kids so they will step out in faith and walk victoriously knowing that the living God will make a way where there seems to be no way, and that they can trust you with their destination. (Joshua 3:14-17)

Live with Hope and Purpose

Heavenly Father, during this month when we celebrate love, may our kids feel your love flood their hearts. Plant a powerful purpose in their hearts and direct their steps. Because you planned their days and created their unique talents, they can trust you completely with every decision. Please give them a burning desire to seek your will and the courage to follow it. Protect them from getting bogged down by activities that keep them too busy to experience the abundant life you want for them and crush any attempt by the enemy to steal their joy or destroy their hope. Lord, give us wisdom so we will be prepared with good advice when it's needed and that we will know when it's more important to stay silent. May our words never interfere with your plan for our kids. (Proverbs 16:9, John 10:10)

Healthy Relationships

Jesus, you modeled what relationships should look like...full of unity, humility, and teamwork. We ask that the relationships of our adult kids be defined by the same qualities. Empower them to show kindness, to be patient, and to be selfless so they will gain the respect of friends and coworkers. Where people cause them emotional pain or put spiritual stumbling blocks in their way, strengthen our kids to walk away. In their marriages, fill them with patience for one another so they will speak kindly and be willing to surrender their own desires for the sake of the team. When stressful situations come, help them to be slow to anger and quick to forgive. Renew their desire to protect one another, to be worthy of trust, to persevere through tough times, and to look forward to the future with common goals. (Ephesians 4:1-6, 1 Corinthians 13:4-7)

Financial Peace

Dear Lord, we know that money can cause stress, so we pray that our adult children will be wise and experience peace in their finances. Just as you gave Joseph wisdom for his daily tasks and the goodwill of his superiors, do the same for our adult kids so they will prosper in their work. May they be diligent in earning an income and even more diligent in how they spend it. Protect them from making idols of money and possessions so they will be protected from debt and greed. Give them the wisdom to seek counsel and to act with integrity when making financial decisions...always being transparent with their spouse. We pray that our kids will joyfully give back to you in such a way that you will throw open the floodgates of heaven and bless them with more than they ever imagined. (Acts 7:9-10, 1 Timothy 6:10, Proverbs 11:3, Malachi 3:10)

Wisdom for Parenting

Jesus, thank you for creating and valuing the grandkids we already have and any that may come in the future. Send your Spirit to speak wisdom into the minds of our adult kids and convict their hearts to make you the first priority in their homes. When our grandkids disobey, teach their parents to discipline them in such a way that their children will grow to bring them honor. We know that parenting is stressful, so we pray that each of our kids will have a sound mind that helps them to discern when to discipline and when to show grace...always remaining calm and patient – especially when they're angry – so our grandkids will learn that God's love is patient and that the purpose of your discipline is always for good. (Matthew 19:14, Exodus 20:3-6, Proverbs 29:15, Proverbs 19:11)

Desire to Know God

Lord, we ask that our kids will have such a great desire to know you and to do your will that their eyes will be open to every temptation; never allowing themselves to be deceived by unhealthy desires. Your Word says that deception leads to sin and that sin results in emotional, spiritual, and even physical death, so we ask your Spirit to prompt our kids to read the Bible. May their love for your Truth, protect them from believing lies that lead to reckless decisions. Make our children aware that they will never experience lasting happiness apart from yourself, and help our kids to learn that their greatest accomplishment on earth will be to know you and to live their lives seeking your steadfast love, justice, and righteousness. (James 1:13-18, Jeremiah 9:23-24)

Emotional and Physical Health

Lord, our kids are faced with so many things that can cause their minds to worry. They are tempted by things that can damage their bodies, and they face challenges that can rob them of joy. We are so thankful that you are holy and that you have authority over every evil thing. Please protect the wellbeing of our kids and send your Spirit to flood their hearts and minds with peace, power, and self-discipline, so they will experience mental, emotional, and physical health. Strengthen them to make choices that glorify you and to walk through hard times with faith and perseverance. You are the one who marks out the race before them, so we ask for you to guide them and to keep their eyes fixed on you. Fill their hearts with so much joy that it overflows to others. (2 Timothy 1:7, 1 Corinthians 10:31, Hebrews 12:1-2, John 17:13)

Now to him who is able to do immeasurably more than all we ask or imagine, according to his power that is at work within us, to him be glory in the church and in Christ Jesus throughout all generations, for ever and ever! Amen. (Ephesians 3:20-21)

"All our infirmities, whatever they are,

are just opportunities for God to display

His gracious work in us."

Charles Spurgeon

MARCH BATTLE PLAN

Focus on Jehovah Rapha: The Lord Who Heals

"He himself bore our sins in his body on the tree;

so that, having died to sins, we might live for righteousness.

By his wounds you have been healed."

1 Peter 2:24

March Agenda

- Fellowship
- Focus on Jehovah Rapha: The Lord Who Heals
- Worship
- Requests & Celebrations
- Prayer

Fellowship Starters

The host can ask these questions while mingling or once everyone is seated:

- At what time of day or night are you most productive?

- What is your favorite kind of cereal?

Focus on Jehovah Rapha: The Lord Who Heals

When the Israelites were dehydrated from wandering in the desert, God heard their cries and provided fresh water, but the water came with this decree:

> *"If you will carefully obey the Lord your God, do what is right in his sight, pay attention to his commands, and keep all his statutes, I will not inflict any illnesses on you...For I am the Lord who heals you."* Exodus 15:26-27

God seems to make it clear that their health and protection are completely dependent on their good behavior. As long as they obeyed all of his commands, then he would heal them.

But what about Job? He was completely obedient; he loved God and turned away from evil, yet God allowed the enemy to destroy Job's entire family, take away every possession, and cover him with painful boils from the soles of his feet to the top of his head (Job 1-2).

And then there's Jesus. He healed many people, even those who were disobedient. He healed the ear of a soldier who came to arrest him and he saved the adulterous woman from being stoned to death. He healed the lame man by the pool of Bethsaida, but left a large number still blind, lame, and paralyzed (John 5:1-9).

Truth is, "The Lord Who Heals" is a mystery to human minds. Though he has the power to heal, he also has the power to allow suffering. We will never make sense of how he works (Isaiah 55:8). We'll never understand why some people get sick and others don't...why some are healed and others aren't. God isn't our Healer because he wants our lives to be convenient, but because he wants to bring glory to himself. And sometimes, greater glory is achieved through suffering.

We live in a sinful world where emotional, mental, and physical pain is inevitable. There's no escaping it. But we also live in a world that was masterfully created by the God of the universe, who is able to end every bit of pain with the whisper of a word...when he wants to. So, how do we reconcile all of this when we're in need of healing?

We run confidently into the arms of the Lord our Healer, knowing that he has the power to take away our pain and trusting that he will answer our prayers in his perfect way. Until healing comes, we meditate on his healing power in scripture, accepting that sometimes he brings glory through healing and sometimes he reveals glory as we wait.

Either way, we are confident that any sickness or injury we suffer in this world will not last. One day, he will wipe every tear from our eyes, and there will be no more death, mourning, crying, or pain. (Revelation 21:4)

Making it Personal

What healing am I praying for in my life or the lives of my kids? Do I really believe that God is *able* to answer my prayer?

_____

_____

_____

How will I bring glory to God while I wait for healing?

_____

_____

_____

How will I respond to God, knowing that he may choose not to heal? (Be honest; he can handle it.)

_____

_____

_____

Worship Songs about the Lord Who Heals:

The following songs may be used to worship God as you prepare your heart to pray. An easy way to find them is to search "Your Soul to Keep Playlist" on Spotify, where the lyrics will scroll for most songs as you listen. If you are going through an especially difficult time, see the "Songs for Extra Hard Days" list on page 301.

- Come Alive (Dry Bones) | Lauren Daigle
- Healer | Casting Crowns
- Healer | Bethel Music, Leah Mari
- The Hurt and the Healer | Mercy Me
- There is Power | Lincoln Brewster

- _____

- _____

March Requests & Celebrations

Use the following pages to record prayer requests and celebrations for each adult child. Remember, no need to fill every box. Simply share as desired.

As you color each space, use it as a guide to direct your prayers.

We run confidently
into the arms of the Lord
our Healer, believing that
he will answer our prayers
in his perfect way.

–Your Soul To Keep–

March Requests & Celebrations for: _____

Consider: Celebrations, Mind, Body, Soul, Career & Finances, Family, Relationships

March Requests & Celebrations for: _____

Consider: Celebrations, Mind, Body, Soul, Career & Finances, Family, Relationships

March Requests & Celebrations for: _____

Consider: Celebrations, Mind, Body, Soul, Career & Finances, Family, Relationships

March Requests & Celebrations for: _____

Consider: Celebrations, Mind, Body, Soul, Career & Finances, Family, Relationships

March Requests & Celebrations for: _____

Consider: Celebrations, Mind, Body, Soul, Career & Finances, Family, Relationships

March Requests & Celebrations for: _____

Consider: Celebrations, Mind, Body, Soul, Career & Finances, Family, Relationships

March Requests & Celebrations for: _____

Consider: Celebrations, Mind, Body, Soul, Career & Finances, Family, Relationships

March Requests & Celebrations for: _____

Consider: Celebrations, Mind, Body, Soul, Career & Finances, Family, Relationships

March Requests & Celebrations for: _____

> Consider: Celebrations, Mind, Body, Soul, Career & Finances, Family, Relationships

March Requests & Celebrations for: _____

> Consider: Celebrations, Mind, Body, Soul, Career & Finances, Family, Relationships

March Requests & Celebrations for: _____

Consider: Celebrations, Mind, Body, Soul, Career & Finances, Family, Relationships

March Requests & Celebrations for: _____

Consider: Celebrations, Mind, Body, Soul, Career & Finances, Family, Relationships

March Requests & Celebrations for: _____

Consider: Celebrations, Mind, Body, Soul, Career & Finances, Family, Relationships

March Requests & Celebrations for: _____

Consider: Celebrations, Mind, Body, Soul, Career & Finances, Family, Relationships

March Requests & Celebrations for: _____

Consider: Celebrations, Mind, Body, Soul, Career & Finances, Family, Relationships

March Requests & Celebrations for: _____

Consider: Celebrations, Mind, Body, Soul, Career & Finances, Family, Relationships

March Requests & Celebrations for: _____

Consider: Celebrations, Mind, Body, Soul, Career & Finances, Family, Relationships

March Requests & Celebrations for: _____

Consider: Celebrations, Mind, Body, Soul, Career & Finances, Family, Relationships

March Requests & Celebrations for: _____

Consider: Celebrations, Mind, Body, Soul, Career & Finances, Family, Relationships

March Requests & Celebrations for: _____

Consider: Celebrations, Mind, Body, Soul, Career & Finances, Family, Relationships

March Prayers

Praising the God Who Heals

Healing Father, we bless your holy name. You forgive offenses and heal diseases. You redeem our lives from the pit and shower us with love and compassion. You heal the brokenhearted and take care of their wounds. You cover us with your feathers so we can take refuge under your wings, and your faithfulness is a shield so we don't have to fear the terror of night. Your faithful love supports us, Lord, when we are filled with cares and anxiety, you comfort us and bring joy. Our flesh and heart may fail, but you give our hearts strength. Your grace is sufficient and your power is made perfect in weakness, so we take pleasure in weakness, hardships, and difficulties for the sake of Christ. For when we are weak, then we are strong. (Psalm 103:1-4, Psalm 147:3, Psalm 91:4-5, Psalm 94:19, Psalm 73:26)

Emotional and Physical Health

Creator of the minds, bodies, and emotions of our kids, we ask that you teach them to set their minds only on what is good and pleasing to you. May they never be governed by the flesh; dragged down by depression or anxiety. Instead, give them spiritual fortitude to surrender fears and negative thoughts to you, so they will experience the abundant life that only you can give. When they can't get there on their own, prompt them to seek help and guide them to professionals who will lead them in your Truth. When healing is needed, increase our faith to be diligent in asking. And when answers seem slow incoming, help us to trust that suffering will produce perseverance, which leads to hope. We love you Lord, we know you love our kids, and we choose to trust you completely. (Romans 8:5-6, Romans 5:3-5)

Protection from Evil

When our kids wrestle with thoughts that are contrary to your truth, remind them that your Spirit provides power to demolish every destructive thought and make it obedient to you. When they're tempted by impure thoughts, teach them how to reject it and walk in holiness. Your Word promises that whoever dwells in your shelter receives protection, so we ask for our kids to recognize you as their faithful shield against evil and to seek you. Protect them from people who want to harm them, from sickness, and from fear. Lord, fill their minds with peaceful thoughts that are focused on eternal things and not on the struggles of this life. You are mighty to save and we ask that you fight for our kids against every form of evil that threatens to harm them. (1 Thessalonians 4:3-5, Psalm 91:1-8, 2 Corinthians 10:5)

Desire to Know God

Father, renew the minds of our kids and open the eyes of their hearts. Guard them against trusting the wisdom of this world so they will only desire your Truth and only seek your will. We pray for them to have the same passion as Daniel, when he refused to stop praying to you...even when it was against the law. May they become passionate about being in your presence and talk with you in prayer every day, even when it seems contrary to logic. Send your Spirit to lead them to your Word so they will pursue thoughts and attitudes that are pleasing to you. Most of all, Jesus, just as you prayed for your children when you were on earth, we pray for our kids to see your glory and to find joy in knowing that you loved them long before the world began. (Romans 12:2, Daniel 6:10, Hebrews 4:12, John 17:24)

Experience God's Power

Lord Jesus, we pray for the minds and bodies of our adult kids to be pierced by your healing power, even at this very moment. Whether the need for healing is known or hidden, touch them with the same power that caused paralyzed people to run...the same power that freed people from seizures, disease, and chronic pain. Just like the servant of the Roman soldier was healed instantly because of his master's faith, we pray that our faith will cause you to heal our kids. Lord, increase our faith! And when your healing power is evident in the minds and bodies of our kids, may it bring glory to you as our generous Healer, so that others will see your works and also have faith in you. (Matthew 4:24, Matthew 8:5-13, John 9:1-7)

Wisdom for Parenting

Perfect Father, you are the author of parenthood and we thank you for every joy it brings. Help us to trust you with every heartache, knowing that you understand and that you're walking through it with us. By the power of your Spirit, instruct our kids in their daily parenting decisions. Make them aware when the busyness of life has caused them to forget you and renew their desire to teach their children about you. Guard their mouths from becoming harsh or unkind. Instead, may their words "always be full of grace, seasoned with salt" so our grandkids will experience your love and grace in their home. Father, protect our kids from the mistakes we made when we were raising them...and protect our grandkids from the mistakes of their parents. By your grace, fill their homes with the knowledge and security of your love. (Deuteronomy 4:9, Colossians 4:6)

Financial Peace

Solomon writes, "When God gives someone wealth and possessions, and the ability to enjoy them, to accept their lot and be happy in their toil—this is a gift of God...he keeps them occupied with gladness of heart." Jesus, we pray that our kids will experience this sort of joy and fulfillment. When they desire things they can't afford, guard them from becoming discontent. Instead, give them wisdom to understand that finding contentment in you is worth far more than anything money can buy, and that being discontent will choke out any joy for the things they already have. Your Word says that you are happy to give good gifts to those who ask, so we boldly ask that you bless our kids with financial stability and the wisdom to be good stewards of all they possess. (Ecclesiastes 5:18-20, Proverbs 8:10-11, Mark 4:19, Matthew 7:11)

Live with Hope and Purpose

Dear Lord, the first time we held our babies in our arms, we wanted their lives to be filled with joy and hope and purpose, and we continue to believe that you have a perfect plan for each of them. May our kids be strengthened by the power of your Spirit, so Christ will dwell in their hearts through faith. When they feel discouraged, motivate them to seek you – their Creator – for hope and direction. If any of them believe that their life isn't valuable, overwhelm them with divine inspiration from your Spirit of Truth. Reveal to them how high and deep your love is for them, and let this revelation cause them to overflow with a sense of hope for the future. Work out your perfect plan for our kids, Lord, and give us the wisdom to know how we should (and shouldn't) be involved in guiding them. (Proverbs 16:3, Ephesians 3:14-21)

Now to him who is able to do immeasurably more than all we ask or imagine, according to his power that is at work within us, to him be glory in the church and in Christ Jesus throughout all generations, for ever and ever! Amen. (Ephesians 3:20-21)

"Just as I am, and waiting not

To rid my soul of one dark blot;

To Thee whose blood can cleanse each spot,

O Lamb of God, I come, I come!"

Charlotte Elliott

APRIL BATTLE PLAN

Focus on Jehovah M'Kaddesh: The Lord Who Sanctifies

"You are to be holy to me because I, the Lord, am holy, and I have set you apart from the nations to be mine."

Leviticus 20:26

April Agenda

- Fellowship
- Focus on Jehovah M'Kaddesh: The Lord Who Sanctifies
- Worship
- Requests & Celebrations
- Prayer

Fellowship Starters

The host can ask these questions while mingling or once everyone is seated:

- What is your favorite bible story?

- If you could permanently eliminate one chore from your to-do list, which would it be?

Focus on Jehovah M'Kaddesh: The Lord Who Sanctifies

"Consecrate yourselves and be holy, for I am the Lord your God. Keep my statutes and do them; I am the Lord who sets you apart...you are to be holy to me because I, the Lord, am holy, and I have set you apart from the nations to be mine." Leviticus 20:7-8, 26

The entire Old Testament is one continual, complicated dance of sanctification between God and his people. Over and over, he reminds them that they are set apart as his treasured possession. Over and over, he reminds them to obey. Over and over they fall short.

The only way to redeem themselves was to adhere to an extensive system of sacrifice and ritual. There was the annual Day of Atonement, when mass rituals served as a symbolic purification of the community from the contamination of sin. Then, there were ongoing personal sacrifices and rituals for sins throughout the year. Just reading about all the requirements is overwhelming because it reveals how utterly impossible it is for any human to achieve holiness on their own.

And then came Jesus; the beautiful Savior who made sinners holy once and for all time. Because of him, we *are* sanctified in God's eyes. Because of the Holy Spirit at work in us, we *continue* to be sanctified, becoming more like Jesus as we grow in wisdom and love. And because we are sanctified, we're set apart for a good and powerful purpose. (Hebrews 10:10, 1 Corinthians 1:30)

It's not a purpose defined by Facebook, TikTok, or the family Christmas card. In fact, it's not defined by human approval of any kind. Let's face it, being a parent is an exercise in humility. We love our kids every day and at every age, but they provide plenty of opportunities for us to question the job we're doing. Even the most obedient children and most Hallmark-like families become objects of judgment, let alone kids and families who are shattered by sin and torn apart by strained relationships.

Every family has heartache, but when we insist on measuring our value by the judgments of others, it can destroy us. We are valued beyond measure, regardless of our circumstances, because we are sanctified by God. We have a good purpose because we are deeply loved and radically forgiven.

So, here's the question: Are the opinions (or the perceived opinions) of others causing stress and anxiety? If so, it's time to stop striving for perfection and start celebrating your value in Christ. It's time to embrace the beautiful truth that you are set apart by God for a good purpose. And it's time to "be transformed by the renewing of your mind, so that you may discern what is the good, pleasing and perfect will of God." (Romans 12:2)

Making it Personal

How does my life reflect gratitude for the saving grace of Jesus? (Not sure if you've received his gift? Visit page 295 to learn more.)

_____

_____

_____

What are things that cause me to feel judged by others? What will I do to remind myself that my value is in Christ alone?

_____

_____

_____

In what ways am I continuing to be sanctified, becoming more like Jesus as I grow in wisdom and love?

_____

_____

_____

Worship Songs About the Lord Who Sanctifies:

The following songs may be used to worship God as you prepare your heart to pray. An easy way to find them is to search "Your Soul to Keep Playlist" on Spotify, where the lyrics will scroll for most songs as you listen. If you are going through an especially difficult time, see the "Songs for Extra Hard Days" list on page 301.

- Amazing Grace (My Chains Are Gone) | Chris Tomlin
- Cross Medley | Anthem Lights
- The Old Rugged Cross | Chris Rice
- Living Hope | Phil Wickham

- _____

- _____

April Requests & Celebrations

Use the following pages to record prayer requests and celebrations for each adult child. Remember, no need to fill every box. Simply share as desired.

As you color each space, use it as a guide to direct your prayers.

LIVE WITH HOPE

JOY

FINANCIAL PEACE

CONTENTMENT

PURPOSE

NEIGHBORS

EXTENDED FAMILY

EMOTIONAL HEALTH

GRANDKIDS

PROTECTION FROM EVIL

WISDOM FOR PARENTING

DESIRE FOR GOD

We are valued beyond measure, regardless of our circumstances, because we are sanctified by God. We have a good purpose because we are deeply loved and radically forgiven by him.

–Your Soul To Keep–

EXPERIENCE GOD'S POWER

HEALTHY RELATIONSHIPS

DISCERNMENT

PRAISE THE LORD WHO SANCTIFIES

PATIENCE

PHYSICAL HEALTH

KIDS

NONBELIEVERS

OUR NATION

PASTORS & MISSIONARIES

April Requests & Celebrations for: _____

Consider: Celebrations, Mind, Body, Soul, Career & Finances, Family, Relationships

April Requests & Celebrations for: _____

Consider: Celebrations, Mind, Body, Soul, Career & Finances, Family, Relationships

April Requests & Celebrations for: _____

Consider: Celebrations, Mind, Body, Soul, Career & Finances, Family, Relationships

April Requests & Celebrations for: _____

Consider: Celebrations, Mind, Body, Soul, Career & Finances, Family, Relationships

April Requests & Celebrations for: _____

Consider: Celebrations, Mind, Body, Soul, Career & Finances, Family, Relationships

April Requests & Celebrations for: _____

Consider: Celebrations, Mind, Body, Soul, Career & Finances, Family, Relationships

April Requests & Celebrations for: _____

Consider: Celebrations, Mind, Body, Soul, Career & Finances, Family, Relationships

April Requests & Celebrations for: _____

Consider: Celebrations, Mind, Body, Soul, Career & Finances, Family, Relationships

April Requests & Celebrations for: _____

Consider: Celebrations, Mind, Body, Soul, Career & Finances, Family, Relationships

April Requests & Celebrations for: _____

Consider: Celebrations, Mind, Body, Soul, Career & Finances, Family, Relationships

April Requests & Celebrations for: _____

Consider: Celebrations, Mind, Body, Soul, Career & Finances, Family, Relationships

April Requests & Celebrations for: _____

Consider: Celebrations, Mind, Body, Soul, Career & Finances, Family, Relationships

April Requests & Celebrations for: _____

Consider: Celebrations, Mind, Body, Soul, Career & Finances, Family, Relationships

April Requests & Celebrations for: _____

Consider: Celebrations, Mind, Body, Soul, Career & Finances, Family, Relationships

April Requests & Celebrations for: _____

Consider: Celebrations, Mind, Body, Soul, Career & Finances, Family, Relationships

April Requests & Celebrations for: _____

Consider: Celebrations, Mind, Body, Soul, Career & Finances, Family, Relationships

April Requests & Celebrations for: _____

Consider: Celebrations, Mind, Body, Soul, Career & Finances, Family, Relationships

April Requests & Celebrations for: _____

Consider: Celebrations, Mind, Body, Soul, Career & Finances, Family, Relationships

April Requests & Celebrations for: _____

Consider: Celebrations, Mind, Body, Soul, Career & Finances, Family, Relationships

April Requests & Celebrations for: _____

Consider: Celebrations, Mind, Body, Soul, Career & Finances, Family, Relationships

April Prayers

Praising the God Who Sanctifies

Our God who sanctifies, we praise you. You sent your son who bore our sins in his own body on the tree, so we might die to sin and live in righteousness. By his wounds we are healed. We seek you with all our hearts and treasure your word in our hearts so that we might not sin against you. Be blessed, Lord, we delight in your ways and will not forget your promises. Our desire is to grow in the grace and knowledge of our Lord and Savior Jesus Christ, who saved us from death and continues to make us holy as we learn to be more like him. To him be the glory both now and to the day of eternity. (1 Peter 2:24, Psalm 119:10-16, 2 Peter 3:18)

Experience God's Power

Dear God, we ask you to powerfully pursue our adult kids. When Jonah ran away from you, you pursued him until he came to his senses; causing him to endure a deadly storm at sea and being swallowed by a great fish. Until finally, Jonah surrendered. Even when Jonah knew that you were the one who threw him into the sea, he praised you because your discipline caused him to wake up from his rebellion and realize that your will for him was far better than his own. Because of his repentance, you rescued him. Lord, pursue the hearts of our kids like you pursued Jonah; reveal disobedience and bring them to their senses. Though we hate to see them suffer, we surrender them into your perfect hands and pray that your discipline causes them to respond with praise. (Jonah 1-2)

Protection from Evil

Father, your Word makes it clear that the hearts of our adult kids can be easily consumed by destructive thoughts, sexual immorality, dishonesty, greed, and foolishness. We invite your Spirit to invade their hearts and minds right now; to convict them of every thought and action that is causing the enemy to have a foothold. Jesus, when they are tempted, be their Defender. Just as Job made a covenant not to look lustfully at a woman, guide our kids to be proactive about guarding themselves against anything displeasing to you. When they are stubborn, willfully choosing to sin, expose what needs to be exposed so they will be brought to repentance. And give us the wisdom to recognize your discipline in their lives, so we will never interfere with their joy being fully restored. (Genesis 8:21, Mark 7:21-22, Psalm 138:7, Job 31:1)

Desire to Know God

Dear Lord, by the power of your Spirit, give our kids a burning desire to know you and to spend time in your presence. May they never be hypocrites, honoring you with their lips while their hearts are far from you. Instead, may they trust you so completely that they will be like well-watered trees that always bear fruit. When life is hard, cause our kids to run to you for help and trust you for answers. We release them into your hands because your power to protect and guide them is far beyond anything we can offer. Jesus, you want our kids to know you, so please send people into their lives who will speak your truth and be examples of your light. Then, open their hearts to receive your love and forgiveness so they will walk in your truth. (Mark 7:6, Jeremiah 17:8, Psalm 20:1-2, John 14:6)

Healthy Relationships

Lord, you are holy...full of compassion and mercy, slow to anger and full of love. Fill our kids with this kind of holiness so they will enjoy healthy relationships. May they have grace for family members, employers, coworkers, neighbors, and friends; forgiving others as you forgive them. Teach our kids to confront conflict with truth that is seasoned with kindness. In the same way, lead our children into relationships with people who will treat them with the same kindness and compassion. By your Spirit, fill their relationships with attitudes that foster unity and words that communicate appreciation. And make them *one flesh* with their spouse as only you can, so they become a beautiful example of Christ's love for the church. (Psalm 103, Colossians 3:13, Ephesians 5:28-29)

Financial Peace

Heavenly Father, protect our kids from putting their confidence in money and becoming arrogant about their possessions. Instead, teach them to put their hope in things that have eternal value. Prompt them to give sacrificially with compassionate hearts, so they will be pleasing to you. In their workplace, may your Spirit motivate them to work with diligence and integrity—as though they are working for you and not for human bosses. And may their labor be rewarded. We pray that our kids will ask for direction before making financial decisions and be protected from unwise choices. Prompt them to seek guidance through prayer and Godly counsel. And if there is any deception in their finances, convict them to confess it and make it right. (1 Timothy 6:10,17, Hebrews 13:16, Colossians 3:23, 1 Corinthians 3:8, Zechariah 8:16)

Live with Hope and Purpose

Oh God, our kids were created according to your will. You knit them together with purpose and we pray that this truth will be revealed to their hearts in a new and powerful way, so they will never question their value. May your Spirit give them a burning desire to seek your wisdom as they make decisions about the future so they will discover their good purpose. When they experience confusion or discouragement, bring clarity. Flood the minds of our kids with life-giving hope this week...hope that is undeniably from you and energizes them to tackle daily responsibilities with a fresh sense of purpose. When they walk down roads that are contrary to your best for them, put angels in their way that cause them to change course. Then give them the desire to listen for your voice directing them somewhere better. (Revelation 4:11, Psalm 139:5-10, Ephesians 1:11)

Emotional and Physical Health

Jesus, your Word says that a *cheerful heart is good medicine* so we pray for our kids to focus on everything good today, and to reject any thoughts that will crush their spirits. Where their bodies are under attack, heal them. Convict them to make decisions that will bring good health to their bodies and their emotions. May your Spirit strengthen them and cause them to develop grit for hard times. When hard times come, we pray that our kids will face them with joy in their hearts, believing that every trial produces perseverance that leads to wisdom. Where their emotions are being attacked by insecurities and fear, we claim your healing power. Wash away every negative thought and make them new so that they will know that you are the only source of peace and contentment. Jesus, wrap them up in your loving arms so that no weapon formed against them will succeed. (Proverbs 17:22, Psalm 41:3, James 1:2-4, 2 Corinthians 5:17, Isaiah 54:17)

Now to him who is able to do immeasurably more than all we ask or imagine, according to his power that is at work within us, to him be glory in the church and in Christ Jesus throughout all generations, for ever and ever! Amen. (Ephesians 3:20-21)

"He has held me when I have had no more strength and have wondered how I would ever make it. He has held me when I have felt defeated by all that I had to do. When I have run to my El Shaddai, I have never come away wanting. He is my all−sufficient One."

Kay Arthur

MAY BATTLE PLAN

Focus on El Shaddai: Lord God Almighty

"Receive instruction from his mouth,

and place his sayings in your heart...

Then you will delight in the Almighty

and lift up your face to God."

Job 22:22, 26

May Agenda

- Fellowship
- Focus on El Shaddai: Lord God Almighty
- Worship
- Requests & Celebrations
- Prayer

Fellowship Starters

The host can ask these questions while mingling or once everyone is seated:

- What has been your favorite road trip or vacation?

- What is one fictional character that you wish was a real person?

Focus on El Shaddai: Lord God Almighty

When Abram was ninety-nine years old, the Lord appeared to him and said, "I am God Almighty (El Shaddai); walk before me faithfully and be blameless. Then I will make my covenant between me and you and will greatly increase your numbers." Genesis 17:1-2

Abraham was 100 years old when God finally gave him the son that was promised 25 years earlier. Twenty. Five. Years.

We get impatient waiting in line for five minutes! And when answers to prayer aren't as swift as we hope, it can cause us to question God. At 99 years old, that's exactly what Abraham does:

...But God, I still don't have a child. (vs. 15:2)
...But God, surely my inheritance will go to a servant. (vs. 15:3)
...But God, how can I believe any of this will happen? (vs. 15:8)
...but God, but God!

Nothing about it made sense, so surely it was time to take matters into his own hands...to help God out. Abraham and his wife begin to plot, with the best intentions, and to find a way for Abraham to have a child with another woman. Then, God's promise will be fulfilled. And soon, Ishmael was born.

But 13 years later, God returned with his original promise, making it clear that Ishmael was not the child God promised. In fact, the promised child would be born to Abraham's wife. His *old* wife. And again, he tries to make sense of it.

> *Abraham fell facedown; he laughed and said to himself,*
> *"Will a son be born to a man a hundred years old? Will Sarah bear*
> *a child at the age of ninety?" And Abraham said to God, "If only*
> *Ishmael might live under your blessing!" (Genesis 17:17-18)*

We are fixers. When circumstances are difficult and confusing in our lives or the lives of our kids, we can get impatient and jump into action, with the best intentions. But what if God has a better plan? What if he wants us to simply be still and *wait* for him to work things out for a greater good?

When Abraham became impatient, God said: "I am El Shaddai; walk before me faithfully and be blameless. Then I will make my covenant..." In other words, *I am in control. Focus on doing what's right and let me take care of the rest.*

El Shaddai has absolute power over every circumstance and every situation. He caused a ninety-year-old woman to give birth and he has the power to provide, supply, nourish, and satisfy our every need...if and when he chooses. When the waiting gets long and your heart can't make sense of it, trust that El Shaddai knows and that he is working things out in his perfect timing.

Making it Personal

What am I continuing to wait for in my life or the lives of my adult children?

_____

_____

_____

In what ways do I find myself plotting to intervene?

_____

_____

_____

Write a prayer, asking God to calm your heart, give you patience as you wait, and increase your trust in him as El Shaddai.

_____

_____

_____

_____

_____

Worship Songs about Our God Almighty:

The following songs may be used to worship God as you prepare your heart to pray. An easy way to find them is to search "Your Soul to Keep Playlist" on Spotify, where the lyrics will scroll for most songs as you listen. If you are going through an especially difficult time, see the "Songs for Extra Hard Days" list on page 301.

- El Shaddai | Amy Grant
- Good God Almighty | Crowder
- Holy Holy Holy | Hillsong UNITED
- Salt & Light | Lauren Daigle

- _____

- _____

May Requests & Celebrations

Use the following pages to record prayer requests and celebrations for each adult child. Remember, no need to fill every box. Simply share as desired.

As you color each space, use it as a guide to direct your prayers.

PATIENCE

EXTENDED FAMILY

LIVE WITH PURPOSE

PHYSICAL HEALTH

HEALTHY RELATIONSHIPS

FINANCIAL PEACE

WISDOM FOR PARENTING

PASTORS & MISSIONARIES

PRAISE GOD ALMIGHTY

NONBELIEVERS

GENTLENESS

PROTECTION FROM EVIL

We sit on a dot of the eternal timeline; looking back to see years past and forward to events and hopes for the future. But the view from our dot is nothing compared to the view of Alpha & Omega from his eternal throne.

−Your Soul To Keep−

DISCERNMENT

LIVE WITH HOPE

NEIGHBORS

JOY & CONTENTMENT

KIDS

EXPERIENCE GOD'S POWER

EMOTIONAL HEALTH

DESIRE FOR GOD

OUR NATION

GRANDKIDS

May Requests & Celebrations for: _____

Consider: Celebrations, Mind, Body, Soul, Career & Finances, Family, Relationships

May Requests & Celebrations for: _____

Consider: Celebrations, Mind, Body, Soul, Career & Finances, Family, Relationships

May Requests & Celebrations for: _____

Consider: Celebrations, Mind, Body, Soul, Career & Finances, Family, Relationships

May Requests & Celebrations for: _____

Consider: Celebrations, Mind, Body, Soul, Career & Finances, Family, Relationships

May Requests & Celebrations for: _____

Consider: Celebrations, Mind, Body, Soul, Career & Finances, Family, Relationships

May Requests & Celebrations for: _____

Consider: Celebrations, Mind, Body, Soul, Career & Finances, Family, Relationships

May Requests & Celebrations for: _____

Consider: Celebrations, Mind, Body, Soul, Career & Finances, Family, Relationships

May Requests & Celebrations for: _____

Consider: Celebrations, Mind, Body, Soul, Career & Finances, Family, Relationships

May Requests & Celebrations for: _____

Consider: Celebrations, Mind, Body, Soul, Career & Finances, Family, Relationships

May Requests & Celebrations for: _____

Consider: Celebrations, Mind, Body, Soul, Career & Finances, Family, Relationships

May Requests & Celebrations for: _____

Consider: Celebrations, Mind, Body, Soul, Career & Finances, Family, Relationships

May Requests & Celebrations for: _____

Consider: Celebrations, Mind, Body, Soul, Career & Finances, Family, Relationships

May Requests & Celebrations for: _____

Consider: Celebrations, Mind, Body, Soul, Career & Finances, Family, Relationships

May Requests & Celebrations for: _____

Consider: Celebrations, Mind, Body, Soul, Career & Finances, Family, Relationships

May Requests & Celebrations for: _____

Consider: Celebrations, Mind, Body, Soul, Career & Finances, Family, Relationships

May Requests & Celebrations for: _____

Consider: Celebrations, Mind, Body, Soul, Career & Finances, Family, Relationships

May Requests & Celebrations for: _____

Consider: Celebrations, Mind, Body, Soul, Career & Finances, Family, Relationships

May Requests & Celebrations for: _____

Consider: Celebrations, Mind, Body, Soul, Career & Finances, Family, Relationships

My Requests & Celebrations for: _____

Consider: Celebrations, Mind, Body, Soul, Career & Finances, Family, Relationships

May Requests & Celebrations for: _____

Consider: Celebrations, Mind, Body, Soul, Career & Finances, Family, Relationships

May Prayers

Praising El Shaddai, God Almighty

Just as David praised you as God Almighty in front of his whole kingdom, we also praise you as the one and only eternal God. You are great in power and glory. Everything in the heavens and on earth belongs to you. Our lives and families are yours and we pray that you are praised as the leader of our steps and the King of our hearts. Riches and honor come from you; you are the ruler of everything. Power and might are in your hand; you give greatness and strength. We desire to serve you and to serve others. Give our children undivided hearts that are fully dedicated to you so they will seek your wisdom and carry out your plan. We give you thanks and praise your glorious name. (David's Prayer: 1 Chronicles 29:10-20)

Experience God's Power

Jesus, awake your resurrection power in the hearts and minds of our adult kids. When Lazarus died, you were troubled by your own grief and troubled by the confusion you saw in others. By the time you arrived at his tomb, it was already filled with the stench of death and still you raised your face to heaven and thanked God in advance for the miracle that was about to take place. Your words defeated death and brought Lazarus out of the tomb, fully alive. At that moment you chose LIFE for him. Right now, we claim that resurrection power for our kids. Where their minds, bodies, or souls are being choked by darkness, bring new light and life to their souls. We raise our faces to you, just as Jesus did, and thank you in advance for your saving power. (John 11:33-40, John 11:41-44, Romans 6:4)

Protection from Evil

Jesus, when you were tempted in the desert the enemy twisted scripture, trying to confuse you, and he does the same thing to our kids. He whispers things that seem right and good but only lead to spiritual and emotional death. Please flood their minds with your Spirit of Truth so they will recognize deception before doing anything that harms themselves or others. Open their eyes to the danger of lustful thoughts and actions so their relationships will be protected and remain pure. Lord, please hear us and bring victory over evil. Help us to trust you completely with our adult kids and to remember that you are the only one who can truly protect them. Fill them with this knowledge so they will turn to you for help when they face spiritual battles of all sorts and trust you as their only deliverer. (Matthew 4, Matthew 5:27-28, Psalm 20:6-8.)

Desire to Know God

Dear Lord, you promise to pour your Spirit into the lives of those who humble themselves. Cause our adult kids to recognize their need for you; may they see that no earthly possession, relationship, accomplishment, or activity will ever satisfy their deepest desires. Where earthly things have become idols, bring our kids to their senses so they know that they will never have hope of worth apart from you. When making decisions about their daily lives, prompt them to pray. Your Word says, "Some trust in chariots and some in horses, but we trust in the name of the Lord." May this be true of our kids so they experience answered prayer that causes them to rise up and stand firm in their faith. If their hearts become hard, humble them so they will never be ashamed of the gospel. Instead, may they find strength and power and purpose in your salvation. (Joel 2:28, Psalm 20:7-9, Romans 1:16)

Healthy Relationships

We pray that the relationships of our adult kids will overflow with Godly love. As spouses, parents, employees, and friends, may their words and actions be examples of your grace, patience, and kindness. Instead of being harsh or rude when they are frustrated, fill their mouths with life-giving words that teach and encourage others. Where our kids are being mistreated by others, give them the strength to say, "Father forgive them, for they don't know what they are doing," and then give them the wisdom and strength to either speak truth or stay silent. In marriage, may our daughters find joy and purpose in submitting to the leadership of their husbands. As they do this, may their husbands respond with gentleness and kindness - loving and protecting their wives as you love and protect your church. (1 Corinthians 13:4, Ephesians 4:26-27, Luke 23:34, Colossians 3:18-19)

Financial Peace

Isaac planted crops that reaped a hundredfold because you blessed him and he became wealthy. Likewise, we pray that our adult kids will experience financial blessing as they strive to be good stewards of their money and material things. Your word says, "Whoever loves money never has enough." Protect our kids from greed so they will be grateful for everything they have and never be defeated by discontentment. By your Spirit, motivate them to work hard every day, not just to accumulate possessions, but to provide for their needs and bless others. Most of all, may they honor you with their finances. Help us to be Godly examples of good stewardship and to honor you with our earthly treasures. (Genesis 26:12-14, Ecclesiastes 5:10)

Live with Hope and Purpose

Dear Jesus, your Word brings encouragement and hope for the future, so we pray that your Holy Spirit will prompt our adult kids to read the Bible and to use it as a tool for making decisions. May they fall in love with your Truth and walk into the future with a strong sense of purpose as they draw near to you. Open their eyes to anyone causing them to wander away from you and from anything robbing them of hope. Please give them the strength to reject anything that isn't *your* best for them. May they see the future with pure eyes and a peaceful heart, free from anxious thoughts, so they will hear your voice directing their steps. Where they feel "stuck" in any situation, penetrate their minds with the desire to press on with diligent and grateful hearts as they wait for you to lead them to something better. (Romans 15:4, Psalm 139:19-24, 1 Thessalonians 5:18)

Wisdom for Parenting

Father, whether our kids are the parents of toddlers or teenagers – or they aren't parents yet - please make them powerfully aware of the importance of raising children with the knowledge that you are their Creator, their wisdom for life, and their hope for eternity. The Bible says that the reward for this type of parenting is the assurance that their children will be grounded in Truth, always returning to you no matter how far they stray. You promise that discipline leads to a harvest of righteousness and peace, so teach our kids to follow through on what they say - never speaking empty threats or ignoring disobedience. And as they discipline, may their words be seasoned with grace so our grandkids begin to understand that they receive discipline for their good and because they are deeply loved. (Proverbs 22:6, Hebrews 12:11, James 2:13)

Now to him who is able to do immeasurably more than all we ask or imagine, according to his power that is at work within us, to him be glory in the church and in Christ Jesus throughout all generations, for ever and ever! Amen. (Ephesians 3:20-21)

"Go about the work as if all depended upon you,

and then trust in God, knowing that all depends upon him."

Charles Spurgeon

JUNE BATTLE PLAN

Focus on Jehovah Nissi: The Lord Is My Banner

"Let us shout for joy at your victory

and lift the banner in the name of our God."

Psalm 20:5

June Agenda

- Fellowship
- Focus on Jehovah Nissi: The Lord Is My Banner
- Worship
- Requests & Celebrations
- Prayer

Fellowship Starters

The host can ask these questions while mingling or once everyone is seated:

- What is the biggest mess you've ever had to clean up?

- What is something you remember about a grandparent?

Focus on Jehovah Nissi: The Lord Is My Banner

"And Moses built an altar and named it, 'The Lord Is My Banner.' He said, "Indeed, my hand is lifted up toward the Lord's throne.'" Exodus 17:15-16

The Israelites escaped slavery in Egypt because God forced Pharaoh to submit. Pharaoh's army was destroyed because God drowned them in the Red Sea. And now Moses and Joshua led God's people in search of the promised land. As they wandered through the wilderness, the people became tired, hungry, thirsty, afraid, and even angry.

About that time, Moses realized that an army of raiders had come to attack them, led by Amalek-the grandson of Esau. There were thousands of men who were well-armed, well-prepared, and determined to defeat the Israelites. It was a grim situation, to say the least. Not only were the Israelites tired and discouraged, it's the first time they had to defend themselves in a battle. And they were not warriors.

Upon realizing the threat, Moses tells Joshua the battle plan: "Select some men for us and go fight against Amalek. Tomorrow I will stand on the hilltop with God's staff in my hand...." (Exodus 17:9)

Can you imagine what Joshua must have been thinking? *Oh okay. I'll go out with a group of weak, complaining men to fight these vicious raiders while you watch the slaughter from the top of the hill. Sounds great.*

In human wisdom, the plan had to sound ridiculous, but we can conclude that the many miracles Joshua had witnessed with his own eyes caused him to trust what Moses said. So, without hesitation, "Joshua did as Moses had told him, and fought against Amalek, while Moses, Aaron, and Hur went up to the top of the hill" (Exodus 17:10).

As Joshua and his men fought with swords, Moses fought with his hands raised in prayer. Each time Moses held his hands up in prayer, the Israelites prevailed. Each time he grew tired and lowered his hands, Amalek prevailed. After many hours, Amalek and his army were defeated by an exhausting mix of courageous fighting and fervent prayer.

Exodus 17:13 reports, "So Joshua defeated Amalek and his army with the sword." True. But the prayer at the top of the hill was a more powerful weapon than the sword that day. God used *both* to bring victory.

Moses recognized that his prayers were important. He recognized the actions of the men who fought were important. And he recognized that only the Lord carried their banner of victory. It's difficult to understand how prayer, God's ordained plan, and human work all fit together. But scripture makes it clear that they DO work together.

Our part, as a soldier of God, is not to make sense of the battle plan. It's to fight hard, pray harder, and trust the Lord our Banner to bring victory.

Making it Personal

Do I tend to rely more on prayer, human works, or God's power to bring victory?

_____

_____

_____

In what specific ways has God provided and guided through life's battles?

_____

_____

_____

How has God used the talents and/or prayers of others to fight my battles or the battles of my kids?

_____

_____

_____

Worship Songs about the God Who Gives Victory

The following songs may be used to worship God as you prepare your heart to pray. An easy way to find them is to search "Your Soul to Keep Playlist" on Spotify, where the lyrics will scroll for most songs as you listen. If you are going through an especially difficult time, see the "Songs for Extra Hard Days" list on page 301.

- God, I Look to You | Bethel Music
- Surrounded (Fight My Battles) | Bethel Music, Kari Jobe
- The Lion and the Lamb | Big Daddy Weave
- Way Maker | Leeland

- _____

- _____

June Requests & Celebrations

Use the following pages to record prayer requests and celebrations for each adult child. Remember, no need to fill every box. Simply share as desired.

As you color each space, use it as a guide to direct your prayers.

FRIENDS & NEIGHBORS

LIVE WITH PURPOSE

KIDS

PASTORS & MISSIONARIES

JOY & CONTENTMENT

PROTECTION FROM EVIL

WISDOM FOR PARENTING

LIVE WITH HOPE

DESIRE FOR GOD

NONBELIEVERS

Our part, as a soldier of God, is not to make sense of the battle plan. It's to fight hard, pray harder, and trust the Lord our Banner to bring victory.

–Your Soul To Keep–

FUTURE

FINANCIAL PEACE

PRAISE JEHOVAH NISSI

PHYSICAL HEALTH

EMOTIONAL HEALTH

GRANDKIDS

EXTENDED FAMILY

HEALTHY RELATIONSHIPS

OUR NATION

EXPERIENCE GOD'S POWER

June Requests & Celebrations for: _____

Consider: Celebrations, Mind, Body, Soul, Career & Finances, Family, Relationships

June Requests & Celebrations for: _____

Consider: Celebrations, Mind, Body, Soul, Career & Finances, Family, Relationships

June Requests & Celebrations for: _____

Consider: Celebrations, Mind, Body, Soul, Career & Finances, Family, Relationships

June Requests & Celebrations for: _____

Consider: Celebrations, Mind, Body, Soul, Career & Finances, Family, Relationships

June Requests & Celebrations for: _____

Consider: Celebrations, Mind, Body, Soul, Career & Finances, Family, Relationships

June Requests & Celebrations for: _____

Consider: Celebrations, Mind, Body, Soul, Career & Finances, Family, Relationships

June Requests & Celebrations for: _____

Consider: Celebrations, Mind, Body, Soul, Career & Finances, Family, Relationships

June Requests & Celebrations for: _____

Consider: Celebrations, Mind, Body, Soul, Career & Finances, Family, Relationships

June Requests & Celebrations for: _____

Consider: Celebrations, Mind, Body, Soul, Career & Finances, Family, Relationships

June Requests & Celebrations for: _____

Consider: Celebrations, Mind, Body, Soul, Career & Finances, Family, Relationships

June Requests & Celebrations for: _____

Consider: Celebrations, Mind, Body, Soul, Career & Finances, Family, Relationships

June Requests & Celebrations for: _____

Consider: Celebrations, Mind, Body, Soul, Career & Finances, Family, Relationships

June Requests & Celebrations for: _____

Consider: Celebrations, Mind, Body, Soul, Career & Finances, Family, Relationships

June Requests & Celebrations for: _____

Consider: Celebrations, Mind, Body, Soul, Career & Finances, Family, Relationships

June Requests & Celebrations for: _____

Consider: Celebrations, Mind, Body, Soul, Career & Finances, Family, Relationships

June Requests & Celebrations for: _____

Consider: Celebrations, Mind, Body, Soul, Career & Finances, Family, Relationships

June Requests & Celebrations for: _____

Consider: Celebrations, Mind, Body, Soul, Career & Finances, Family, Relationships

June Requests & Celebrations for: _____

Consider: Celebrations, Mind, Body, Soul, Career & Finances, Family, Relationships

June Requests & Celebrations for: _____

Consider: Celebrations, Mind, Body, Soul, Career & Finances, Family, Relationships

June Requests & Celebrations for: _____

Consider: Celebrations, Mind, Body, Soul, Career & Finances, Family, Relationships

June Prayers

Praising the Lord our Banner

Our Lord who gives victory, just as Moses lifted his hands to heaven, we lift our hearts toward you. Just as Joshua ran onto the battlefield armed with a sword, we arm ourselves with the sword of your Spirit. Go before us onto the battlefield as we fight for our adult kids. When the enemy pursues them, teach our kids to fight with the Truth of your Word, to behave in ways that are pleasing to you, and to follow your voice into battle. Help us, Lord, to fight for our kids tirelessly in prayer, as Moses did, and to trust you for victory no matter how grim it seems. When our kids reject you or wander away from your path, send your Spirit to pierce their hearts. Remind them that you are their Creator, that you have a perfect plan for their lives, and that you are their only hope of victory. (Exodus 17)

Healthy Relationships

Lord, lead our kids to relationships that are healthy and uplifting. You say that wise friends make us wise and that foolish friends make us foolish. Plant wisdom in our kids so they will choose to spend time with people who are wise according to your Word. We pray that they will never be controlled by pride, but that they will be kind and generous. Fill them with the same love and empathy that Jesus modeled on earth. In marriage, teach our sons to love with patience and to be protectors. Teach our daughters to act and speak respectfully so their marriages will be filled with tenderness. As we continue learning how to be parents of adult children, fill us with wisdom so that our own words and actions never interfere with the work you are doing in their relationships. (Proverbs 13:20, 1 Peter 3:8, Ephesians 5:33)

Experience God's Power

Lord, we invite your power of provision into the lives of our adult kids. Your Word tells of a widow who cried in fear because of debt. But you told her to use the small amount of oil she already had to fill many jars. It made no sense, but she acted quickly and you caused the oil to multiply as she filled jar after jar. When every empty jar was full, she sold the oil to pay her debts and she had enough left over to live in abundance. Generous God, we pray that our kids will also act quickly to follow your instruction so they will experience powerful provision in their lives. May they trust you with every material need, surrendering everything they have to you. And when blessings come, may they fall before you with grateful hearts. (2 Kings 4:2-7)

Desire to Know God

Father, plant a desire in the hearts of our kids to engage in a church so they won't be tossed around by worldly wisdom or pulled into relationships that cause them to stray from you. Help them to see that going to church will increase wisdom for life and love for others. May your Spirit cause them to seek you above everything else and to fall in love with your Word. We pray they will walk in Truth and stand firm when life is hard. By your grace, bring salvation to all of our children and instruct them to live in a sensible, righteous, and godly way. Fill them with your presence and surround them with people who will point them to you, so that your salvation will cause them to put their hope in you. (Ephesians 4:14-16, Matthew 7:24-27, Titus 2:11-14)

Financial Peace

The cattle on a thousand hills are yours, Father, and everything in the world belongs to you. Just as you caused the widow's jars to overflow with oil, cause our kids to overflow with wisdom and in favor with people. Grant them work that is satisfying, profitable, and pleasing to you. And may they work hard to provide for themselves and their families, yet stay away from the love of money so they will have sincere gratitude for the homes they live in, the cars they drive, and the possessions they own. Make their hearts content. You say that the plans of the diligent lead to profit as surely as being reckless leads to poverty. Lord, intervene when our kids are impulsive with their finances so they will learn the value of saving, investing, and making responsible decisions that lead to financial peace. (Psalm 50:10-14, Luke 2:52, Psalm 90:17, 1 Timothy 6:10, Proverbs 21:5)

Protection from Evil

According to your Word, cause our adult kids to desire only what is true, honorable, pure, and lovely. Fill their minds with what is excellent and worthy of praise so their hearts will be guarded with peace. Jesus, we pray that you surround our kids with protection and crush any attempt by the enemy to distract or deceive them. We know that you were tempted by things that seemed good, but you did not sin, so we pray that you will also help our kids to reject temptation...even when it seems harmless to them. Speak into their hearts so they will know that you empathize with them when they fail, and that your grace gives them the strength to reject the lies of shame and guilt. Because of your great love, your mercies never end. Thank you for loving our children every day and for your great faithfulness. (Philippians 4:8, Hebrews 4:15, 1 Corinthians 10:13, Lamentations 3:22-23)

Emotional and Physical Health

Father, you already know the emotional burdens our kids carry so we pray that they will run to you for relief and lay every worry at your feet. May they pay attention to you and treasure your Word in their hearts so it will bring health to their bodies and life to their souls. By your Spirit, teach our kids that their bodies are your temple and should be used to honor you. Strengthen them to make healthy decisions that lead to good health and abundant life. Just as Jesus did on earth, heal the minds of our kids of any anxiety or depression from the enemy. You are their Creator and everlasting God who never grows tired or weary, so we pray that they will fall into your arms when they are tired or discouraged and trust you to renew their strength. (Proverbs 4:17-22, 1 Corinthians 6:19-20, Acts 10:38, Isaiah 30:28-29)

Wisdom for Parenting

Heavenly Father, wrap your arms around our grandkids and fill them with an understanding of your kingdom. We pray for your Spirit to flood the hearts and minds of our adult kids with passion to train their children in the way they should go by talking about you in their homes, praying as a family, and going to church. Teach our kids to love their children with mercy, kindness, and discipline so that our grandkids will have living examples of godly love. Teach our kids to guide our grandkids through today's corrupt culture so they will be protected from anything contrary to your Truth, and they will shine like stars in a dark world. For our future grandchildren, we pray for your perfect timing and your perfect will to be done, just as it was for Isaac. Give us wisdom to support our adult kids in their parenting journey with wisdom, grace, and Truth. (Matthew 19:13-14, Proverbs 22:6, Luke 6:36, Hebrews 12:6, Philippians 2:15, Genesis 21:1)

Now to him who is able to do immeasurably more than all we ask or imagine, according to his power that is at work within us, to him be glory in the church and in Christ Jesus throughout all generations, for ever and ever! Amen. (Ephesians 3:20-21)

"God cannot give us a happiness and peace apart from Himself, because it is not there. There is no such thing."

C.S. Lewis

JULY BATTLE PLAN

Focus on Jehovah Shalom: The Lord Is Peace

"Don't worry about anything, but in everything,

through prayer and petition with thanksgiving,

present your requests to God. And the peace of God,

which surpasses all understanding, will guard

your hearts and minds in Christ Jesus."

Philippians 6:6-7

July Agenda

- Fellowship
- Focus on Jehovah Shalom: The Lord Is Peace
- Worship
- Requests & Celebrations
- Prayer

Fellowship Starters

The host can ask these questions while mingling or once everyone is seated:

- Which would be more difficult for you to go a week without: A cell phone or your personal vehicle?

- What bible story do you wish you could have witnessed?

Focus on Jehovah Shalom: The Lord Is Peace

"...Gideon replied, 'but if the Lord is with us, why has all this happened to us? Where are all his wonders that our ancestors told us about...The Lord turned to him and said, 'Go in the strength you have and save Israel out of Midian's hand...I will be with you, and you will strike down all the Midianites....Peace! Do not be afraid. You are not going to die.'" Judges 6:1-23

Jehovah Shalom occurs once in scripture. And it comes in the midst of great fear, oppression, and need. It comes in the seventh year of the Israelites being dominated by the Midianites...like bloody scenes snatched from the pages of a Vikings novel. It comes in the midst of it; not when it's over.

When God's angel appears to Gideon - an ordinary man, angry about his current reality - Gideon doesn't throw his hands up and walk away. No, instead he pursues truth with an honest and passionate heart. "If the Lord is with us, why has all this happened?" Isn't it the same question we ask when our country is in chaos, our health fails, and our hearts ache?

God, where are you?

The Lord isn't surprised or offended by Gideon's response. He doesn't blast him for lacking faith. He simply says, "The Lord is with you, mighty warrior...Go in the strength that you have."

And Gideon laughs. Well, not actually but his response is pretty funny. "Pardon me...how can I save Israel? My clan is the weakest...and I am the least in my family?" In other words: *Seriously, anyone else is better for the job, Lord. Anyone else.*

But God continues to reassure him. He promises to be with him and confirms that the time is right. Gideon, still unsure, tests the message to be sure he is hearing from God himself...and not being deceived. When confirmation comes, Gideon finds the passion to carry out his calling. And the peace to fight.

"Gideon built an altar to the Lord there and called it The Lord Is Peace." Judges 6:24

What problems make you angry? Do you ever feel like your world is falling apart...like God has forgotten you? Do you feel inadequate? Cry out to Jehovah Shalom - our Lord of Peace. In his presence, there is no strife. There is no fear. Only the promise of comfort and strength and victory.

Being a Christian doesn't save us from war. It arms us with everything we need to fight valiantly. To endure loss. And to persevere with peace in our hearts.

Our message from Jesus is this: "I have told you these things, so that in me you may have peace. In this world you will have trouble. But take heart! I have overcome the world." John 16:33

Making it Personal

Have I ever felt like Gideon when he cried, "if the Lord is with us, why has all this happened to us?" What circumstances have caused me to feel that way?

_____

_____

_____

Gideon didn't hold his frustrations back from God. What fears, frustrations, and questions do I need to share with God today?

_____

_____

_____

After listening to God's assurance, Gideon was finally able to embrace him as the Lord of Peace. What assurance from God's Word do I need to focus on this week?

_____

_____

_____

Worship Songs about the Lord of Peace:

The following songs may be used to worship God as you prepare your heart to pray. An easy way to find them is to search "Your Soul to Keep Playlist" on Spotify, where the lyrics will scroll for most songs as you listen. If you are going through an especially difficult time, see the "Songs for Extra Hard Days" list on page 301.

- God of Peace (acoustic) | Nikki Moltz, Josh Barnett
- It Is Well with My Soul | Joey + Rory
- Leaning On the Everlasting Arms | Selah
- Tremble | Mosaic MSC

- _____

- _____

July Requests & Celebrations

Use the following pages to record prayer requests and celebrations for each adult child. Remember, no need to fill every box. Simply share as desired.

As you color each space, use it as a guide to direct your prayers.

EMOTIONAL HEALTH

PATIENCE

DESIRE FOR GOD

LIVE WITH HOPE

OUR NATION

FRIENDS & NEIGHBORS

GRANDKIDS

EXTENDED FAMILY

WISDOM FOR PARENTING

NONBELIEVERS

KIDS

EXPERIENCE GOD'S POWER

JOY & CONTENTMENT

Being a Christian doesn't save us from war. It arms us with everything we need to fight valiantly. To endure loss. And to persevere with peace in our hearts.

−Your Soul To Keep−

PROTECTION FROM EVIL

HEALTHY RELATIONSHIPS

LIVE WITH PURPOSE

PRAISE THE GOD OF PEACE

FINANCIAL PEACE

PHYSICAL HEALTH

PASTORS & MISSIONARIES

GENTLENESS

DISCERNMENT

July Requests & Celebrations for: _____

Consider: Celebrations, Mind, Body, Soul, Career & Finances, Family, Relationships

July Requests & Celebrations for: _____

Consider: Celebrations, Mind, Body, Soul, Career & Finances, Family, Relationships

July Requests & Celebrations for: _____

Consider: Celebrations, Mind, Body, Soul, Career & Finances, Family, Relationships

July Requests & Celebrations for: _____

Consider: Celebrations, Mind, Body, Soul, Career & Finances, Family, Relationships

July Requests & Celebrations for: _____

Consider: Celebrations, Mind, Body, Soul, Career & Finances, Family, Relationships

July Requests & Celebrations for: _____

Consider: Celebrations, Mind, Body, Soul, Career & Finances, Family, Relationships

July Requests & Celebrations for: _____

Consider: Celebrations, Mind, Body, Soul, Career & Finances, Family, Relationships

July Requests & Celebrations for: _____

Consider: Celebrations, Mind, Body, Soul, Career & Finances, Family, Relationships

July Requests & Celebrations for: _____

Consider: Celebrations, Mind, Body, Soul, Career & Finances, Family, Relationships

July Requests & Celebrations for: _____

Consider: Celebrations, Mind, Body, Soul, Career & Finances, Family, Relationships

July Requests & Celebrations for: _____

Consider: Celebrations, Mind, Body, Soul, Career & Finances, Family, Relationships

July Requests & Celebrations for: _____

Consider: Celebrations, Mind, Body, Soul, Career & Finances, Family, Relationships

July Requests & Celebrations for: _____

Consider: Celebrations, Mind, Body, Soul, Career & Finances, Family, Relationships

July Requests & Celebrations for: _____

Consider: Celebrations, Mind, Body, Soul, Career & Finances, Family, Relationships

July Requests & Celebrations for: _____

Consider: Celebrations, Mind, Body, Soul, Career & Finances, Family, Relationships

July Requests & Celebrations for: _____

Consider: Celebrations, Mind, Body, Soul, Career & Finances, Family, Relationships

July Requests & Celebrations for: _____

Consider: Celebrations, Mind, Body, Soul, Career & Finances, Family, Relationships

July Requests & Celebrations for: _____

Consider: Celebrations, Mind, Body, Soul, Career & Finances, Family, Relationships

July Requests & Celebrations for: _____

Consider: Celebrations, Mind, Body, Soul, Career & Finances, Family, Relationships

July Requests & Celebrations for: _____

Consider: Celebrations, Mind, Body, Soul, Career & Finances, Family, Relationships

July Prayers

Praising the Lord of Peace

Lord of Peace, equip me for battle and be with me. May my soul find rest in you, my rock and my salvation, because you are my fortress. I will never be shaken. Even when life is hard and there are heartbreaking battles to fight, I will choose to find rest and hope in you. I will pour my heart out to you and pursue your Truth with passion. This life is like a fleeting breath but you endure forever. May I never fill my heart with earthly treasure or put my hope in human strength. Power belongs to you, God, and you never fail. Only you bring victory in the battle. Only you give me the power to survive tough times. Only you are my peace. (Psalm 62)

Protection from Evil

Summer is such a fun season; bless our kids with special moments that revive their souls and deepen family connections. At the same time, protect them from worldly influences and from developing wrong priorities that focus only on entertainment and pleasure. When our kids travel, remove anything in their way that is intended to cause harm. Send your angels ahead of them to guard their way and take them safely to their destination. And when they're away from home, guard their hearts with all vigilance and keep them from temptation so they will experience abundant life and spread everywhere the sweet aroma of the knowledge of you. Lord, just as you rescued the Israelites from their enemies, rescue our kids from anyone with malicious intentions and surround them with people who are helpful and kind. (Exodus 23:20, Proverbs 4:23, 2 Corinthians 2:14, 2 Kings 13:5)

Desire to Know God

As we celebrate freedom, help our kids develop a deep desire for the freedom only you can give; freedom from the consequences of sin and the fear of death. May they declare with their mouths that you are Lord and believe in their hearts that you raised Jesus from the dead so they will be saved from the bondage of this world. As they walk in freedom, draw them into your presence, teach them to pray, and to seek your Word for direction. When our kids don't appear to make church a priority, we pray that you will renew their desire for Christian community. Give us wisdom as we seek to be good examples of obedience to your Word. May our lives inspire our kids to love you more, to seek you more, and to understand that being a Christian isn't about being "good" but about loving you and desiring to follow your Word. (Romans 8:21, Romans 10:9-10)

Experience God's Power

The Israelites were held captive in Egypt for decades, enduring "bitter and hard labor" that left them "broken in spirit." They were stuck in a cruel situation with little hope of ever being free. Still, you were there. You saw their pain, you continued to love them, and you had a plan...even when they couldn't see it. After hundreds of years, you led them out of slavery; displaying your power at every obstacle. When they didn't know where to go, you sent a pillar of fire to guide them. When the Red Sea blocked them from safety, you made a way. Over and over, your power made a way out of captivity. Lord, we claim this same power in the lives of our adult kids. Where they are held captive by strongholds, set them free. And where they are lost, guide them. (Exodus 1:14, 6:9, Exodus 13:21, Exodus 14:21)

Healthy Relationships

Father, our parenting role has changed so much since our children were young, and it continues to change as the years go on. By your Spirit, give us the wisdom to "parent" well and the strength to release our adult kids into your hands every day. Forgive us for words and actions that have caused our kids to stumble or caused our relationship with them to be out of line with your plan. Just as you loved and guided Joseph, love and guide our kids. Just as Joseph was a servant, move the hands and feet of our kids to serve others. Just as Joseph rejected inappropriate relationships, guide our kids to the right people so they will experience healthy relationships that honor you. As Joseph was wise in how he dealt with others, plant wisdom in the minds of our kids so they will receive favor. (Genesis 39:21-23, Genesis 39:11-12)

Live with Hope and Purpose

Lord God, you revealed a beautiful purpose for Joseph; reveal your beautiful purpose for each of our adult kids also. So many things went wrong for Joseph. He was betrayed, beaten, and imprisoned, but each obstacle caused him to grow strong in character and in faith. Though the enemy had plans to harm him, you turned it all to good. We pray the same for our kids. Move their hearts to seek your direction when they feel stuck in darkness. Shine light on their path and give them a clear sense of purpose. When they feel lost, grow good character and faith. And crush any attempt by the enemy to rob them of the confidence that you began a good work in them before they were even born. Thank you for creating each of our kids purposefully, for loving them, and for promising to complete the good work you've started. (Genesis 50:20, Psalm 139:11-12, Philippians 1:6)

Wisdom for Parenting

Father, thank you for the grandkids we already have and for any we may have in the future. They are such a treasure and we pray that their parents will raise them with wisdom and love. Help our kids to understand that loving you with all of their heart, all of their soul, and all of their mind is the greatest thing they can do for their kids. When our grandkids are disobedient or unkind, may they receive discipline that honors you and leads to good character. Fill our adult kids with your Holy Spirit so they will demonstrate the wisdom of patience and gentleness, and resist the urge to respond harshly or in anger. More than anything, we ask that our kids will live lives that set an example of all that is good; full of integrity, discernment, and wise words so that our grandkids will learn to value behavior that reflects Jesus. (Matthew 22:37-38, Proverbs 15:1, Titus 2:7-8)

Emotional and Physical Health

Jesus, when our kids are discouraged or have anxious thoughts, give them the assurance that all who are weary and burdened can find rest in you. Send your Spirit to invade their hearts and minds, flooding them with the overwhelming desire to come to you for help. Teach them to have grit for hard times and to recognize you as their only source of renewed strength and freedom to soar. When their bodies are sick or hurt, intervene as their great Healer; restore their health and heal their wounds. Open the eyes of our kids to any habits causing harm to their bodies or minds. Convict them to make difficult changes and surround them with people who will support those changes. Lord, when we need to speak up, give us the right words to say. When we need to stay silent, put a guard over our mouths. We surrender their health to you. (Matthew 11:28, Isaiah 40:30-31, Jeremiah 30:17)

Now to him who is able to do immeasurably more than all we ask or imagine, according to his power that is at work within us, to him be glory in the church and in Christ Jesus throughout all generations, for ever and ever! Amen. (Ephesians 3:20-21)

"Good soldiers know that if they don't recognize who their enemy is, they are destined to lose the war. That is also true for those of us who battle in God's army."

Stormie Omartian

AUGUST BATTLE PLAN

Focus on Jehovah Sabaoth: The Lord of Armies

"You come against me with a sword, spear,

and javelin, but I come against you in the name of the

Lord of Armies, the God of the ranks of Israel."

1 Samuel 17:45

August Agenda

- Fellowship
- Focus on Jehovah Sabaoth: The Lord of Armies
- Worship
- Requests & Celebrations
- Prayer

Fellowship Starters

The host can ask these questions while mingling or once everyone is seated:

- What was the worst style choice you ever made?
- What's your favorite kind of sandwich?

Focus on Jehovah Sabaoth: The Lord of Armies

When David stood before Goliath holding five stones and a slingshot, he shouted, *"You come against me with a sword, spear, and javelin, but I come against you in the name of the **Lord of Armies**, the God of the ranks of Israel—you have defied him. Today, the Lord will hand you over to me...Then all the world will know that Israel has a God, and this whole assembly will know that it is not by sword or by spear that the Lord saves, for the battle is the Lord's."* 1 Samuel 17:45-47

It's a warrior's speech that conjures up scenes from our favorite movies. It's bold and confident and filled with adrenaline. It's a salute to the power of Jehovah Sabaoth, our Lord of Armies.

Sabaoth means *God who reigns over heaven and earth*; over armies, angels, and the stars of the universe. Jehovah Sabaoth is mighty and powerful and supreme.

But the Lord of Armies also reigns in quiet rooms...in tired souls and broken hearts.

In fact, the first time this name of God appears in scripture, it doesn't come from a warrior or an angel, and it doesn't boom down from heaven in Hollywood fashion. It comes from the agonizing cries of Hannah; a wounded woman who longed for a child but was unable to conceive.

She was loved deeply by her husband but he struggled to understand why her pain was so bitter. Year after year, he prayed for her to have a child, but year after year the Lord closed her womb.

On her darkest day, scripture says that Hannah prayed with a broken heart, from the depth of anguish and resentment, "Lord of Armies, if you will take notice of your servant's affliction, remember and not forget me, and give your servant a son, I will give him to the Lord all the days of his life...'" (1 Samuel 1:9-11)

It's a prayer to Jehovah Sabaoth from a shattered heart. But that's not the end of her story. The Lord hears her cries, opens her womb, and Hannah gives birth to Samuel who becomes one of the great spiritual leaders of Israel. We're never told why God kept her from conceiving or why she endured such bitter pain. All we're told is that the Lord answered her prayer.

Hannah's story shows us that God isn't just the Lord of mighty warriors. He is the Lord of the tired and broken. And he hears us. In the midst of public battles or private pain, the Lord of Armies has supreme authority to intervene.

Are your adult kids fighting big battles with bold and courageous hearts? Or are they broken with pain, just trying to survive? Whether their battles are being fought boldly or in brokenness, cry out to the Lord of Armies on their behalf and believe that he hears you. He cares. And he is able.

Making it Personal

What prayer do I find myself praying year after year? If there isn't one yet, is there something I should be praying persistently for?

_____

_____

_____

Do I struggle to understand why God continues to allow pain and struggle in the life of an adult child? What do I need to tell the Lord of Armies about my struggle?

_____

_____

_____

What encouragement do I feel in response to Hannah's story in 1 Samuel 1:1–28?

_____

_____

_____

Worship Songs About the Lord of Armies:

The following songs may be used to worship God as you prepare your heart to pray. An easy way to find them is to search "Your Soul to Keep Playlist" on Spotify, where the lyrics will scroll for most songs as you listen. If you are going through an especially difficult time, see the "Songs for Extra Hard Days" list on page 301.

- I Will Fear No More | The Afters
- Lift My Eyes | Alisa Turner
- Mighty to Save |Hillsong Worship
- Whom Shall I Fear (Angel Armies) | Chris Tomlin

- _____

- _____

August Requests & Celebrations

Use the following pages to record prayer requests and celebrations for each adult child. Remember, no need to fill every box. Simply share as desired.

As you color each space, use it as a guide to direct your prayers.

God isn't just the Lord of mighty warriors. He is the Lord of the tired and broken. And he hears us. In the midst of public battles and private pain, the Lord of Armies has supreme authority to intervene.

-Your Soul To Keep-

NONBELIEVERS

PRAISE THE LORD OF ARMIES

FINANCIAL PEACE

OUR NATION

GRANDKIDS

NEIGHBORS & FRIENDS

DESIRE FOR GOD

PROTECTION FROM EVIL

LIVE WITH PURPOSE

WISDOM FOR PARENTING

PASTORS & MISSIONARIES

EXPERIENCE GOD'S POWER

KIDS

LIVE WITH HOPE

EMOTIONAL HEALTH

PHYSICAL HEALTH

HEALTHY RELATIONSHIPS

CONTENTMENT

GRACE

EXTENDED FAMILY

August Requests & Celebrations for: _____

Consider: Celebrations, Mind, Body, Soul, Career & Finances, Family, Relationships

August Requests & Celebrations for: _____

Consider: Celebrations, Mind, Body, Soul, Career & Finances, Family, Relationships

August Requests & Celebrations for: _____

Consider: Celebrations, Mind, Body, Soul, Career & Finances, Family, Relationships

August Requests & Celebrations for: _____

Consider: Celebrations, Mind, Body, Soul, Career & Finances, Family, Relationships

August Requests & Celebrations for: _____

Consider: Celebrations, Mind, Body, Soul, Career & Finances, Family, Relationships

August Requests & Celebrations for: _____

Consider: Celebrations, Mind, Body, Soul, Career & Finances, Family, Relationships

August Requests & Celebrations for: _____

Consider: Celebrations, Mind, Body, Soul, Career & Finances, Family, Relationships

August Requests & Celebrations for: _____

Consider: Celebrations, Mind, Body, Soul, Career & Finances, Family, Relationships

August Requests & Celebrations for: _____

Consider: Celebrations, Mind, Body, Soul, Career & Finances, Family, Relationships

August Requests & Celebrations for: _____

Consider: Celebrations, Mind, Body, Soul, Career & Finances, Family, Relationships

August Requests & Celebrations for: _____

Consider: Celebrations, Mind, Body, Soul, Career & Finances, Family, Relationships

August Requests & Celebrations for: _____

Consider: Celebrations, Mind, Body, Soul, Career & Finances, Family, Relationships

August Requests & Celebrations for: _____

Consider: Celebrations, Mind, Body, Soul, Career & Finances, Family, Relationships

August Requests & Celebrations for: _____

Consider: Celebrations, Mind, Body, Soul, Career & Finances, Family, Relationships

August Requests & Celebrations for: _____

Consider: Celebrations, Mind, Body, Soul, Career & Finances, Family, Relationships

August Requests & Celebrations for: _____

Consider: Celebrations, Mind, Body, Soul, Career & Finances, Family, Relationships

August Requests & Celebrations for: _____

Consider: Celebrations, Mind, Body, Soul, Career & Finances, Family, Relationships

August Requests & Celebrations for: _____

Consider: Celebrations, Mind, Body, Soul, Career & Finances, Family, Relationships

August Requests & Celebrations for: _____

Consider: Celebrations, Mind, Body, Soul, Career & Finances, Family, Relationships

August Requests & Celebrations for: _____

Consider: Celebrations, Mind, Body, Soul, Career & Finances, Family, Relationships

August Prayers

Praising the Lord of Armies

Lord of Armies, you are our refuge and strength; a helper who can always be found in times of trouble. Even if the earth trembles and the mountains fall, we will not be afraid. Nations rage and the earth melts when you raise your voice. The Lord of Armies is with us and is our stronghold. You make wars cease throughout the earth. You shatter every weapon that is raised against us. You say to stop fighting and to know that you are God. You are the king of Heaven and Earth and you are with us. When we face battles that are bigger than us, we will not be afraid of them because the Lord of Armies is with us; our hearts will not faint and we will not panic because you go with us and fight for us. We proclaim the Lord's greatness and praise your name together. (Psalm 46, Deuteronomy 20:1-4, Psalm 34:3)

Healthy Relationships

Father, you teach us to love each other and warn that fighting against each other will destroy us. Our world is flooded with hate and selfish ambition, putting our own needs before the needs of others. Destroy this message in the hearts of our kids so they will love others with the same love and humility that Jesus demonstrated while he was on earth. Destroy rudeness and guard them against "keeping score" with their spouse. Instead, fill their hearts with love, humility, and a desire for peace. When our kids are tempted to say rude or hurtful things, close their lips so the only words they speak are helpful for building others up. And may they faithfully love their families, never allowing anything to undermine the love they have for one another. (Galatians 5:14-25, Galatians 5:22-26)

Protection from Evil

Jesus, we believe you love our adult kids and that you have a great purpose for each one. Command your angels concerning them and guard them in all their ways. May they love you and call on you to fight for them, so they will experience your protection in times of trouble. Bless them with long life and protect them from immorality, evil desires, jealousy, and idolatry. Crush every attempt by the enemy to trap our kids into chasing temporary pleasures that will only disappoint. By your Spirit, cause them to be passionate about using your truth as a weapon against temptation and a compass to lead them to a healthy and fulfilled life. When anyone tries to persuade our kids away from Truth, open their eyes to it so they will never walk away from you. (Psalm 91:11-16, Colossians 3:5, Galatians 5:7-10)

Experience God's Power

Lord, you showed your power to fight for us thousands of years ago, when the king of Babylon commanded all people to worship a golden image. If they didn't, they would be killed. When three men refused, the king had them bound and thrown into a fire to die. Even though it seemed hopeless, the men believed you would rescue them, and because of their faith you fought for them. By your power, the flames did not consume them. The Bible says they were in the fire "unbound and unharmed." We ask for you to grow this kind of faith in our kids. And by your Spirit, give them the desire and strength to honor you by the way they live so that your saving power is unleashed in their lives. Stand with them in their *fires* so they will walk through them unbound and unharmed. (Daniel 3)

Financial Peace

Lord, thank you for the promise that we can enjoy our work and never labor in vain. Plant this attitude in our adult kids so they will find joy in whatever job is paying their bills. When they work hard to provide for themselves, reward their efforts by meeting their needs according to your glorious riches. When they feel discontent, open their eyes to the freedom they can find in a grateful heart. Even in their darkest financial times, help them to find things to be thankful for. When making financial decisions, send your Spirit to counsel our kids so they will always calculate the cost first and never buy things that lead to a bondage of debt. Help us to be excellent examples of what it looks like to be good stewards of our money and possessions so we will never cause our kids to stumble. (Isaiah 65:22-23, Philippians 4:19, 1 Thessalonians 5:18, Luke 14:28, Romans 13:14)

Live with Hope and Purpose

In your mercy, you give living hope through the resurrection of Jesus Christ, and grant us an inheritance that will never perish, spoil or fade. Thank you so much for this promise! We pray that it pierces the hearts of our kids so they will find hope for the future and truly believe that their purpose far exceeds the temporary pain of this life. Fill them with inspiration from your Spirit so they will have a strong sense of direction and never be held back by insecurity or fear. Help our kids to rejoice when things go well, to be patient in trials, and to be persistent in prayer for their future. Jesus, stop us from interfering with your work in the lives of our kids. And give us the emotional strength to release everything into your hands, knowing you are in control. (1 Peter 1:3-4, Romans 12:12)

Wisdom for Parenting

Heavenly Father, teach our adult children to parent their kids with purpose and by example. When our grandkids misbehave, convict our kids of the importance of discipline. You promise that discipline leads to peace and righteousness, so teach our kids to raise our grandkids in a way that they will learn that Godly discipline is compassionate, patient, and life-giving. We pray for any future grandchildren we may have; for knitting them together perfectly and ordaining their days before they're even born. Guard the health and minds of our daughters during pregnancy and delivery. Teach our sons to be wise and kind fathers who are examples of Godly love to their families. And prepare our adult kids to be parents who are pleasing to you. (Hebrews 12:11, Colossians 3:12)

Emotional and Physical Health

Lord, your Word says, "Blessed is the one who trusts in the Lord, whose confidence is in him. They will be like a tree planted by the water that sends out its roots by the stream. It does not fear when heat comes; its leaves are always green. It has no worries in a year of drought and never fails to bear fruit." What a beautiful picture of what we want life to be like for our adult kids. Please speak this truth into their hearts so they will put their confidence in you, even on the darkest days. Heal their emotional hurts, remove fear and anxiety, and crush any lies that cause them to feel discouraged. You are the God of sound minds. Thank you for the hope that you will restore our kids when they have faced trials and make them strong. (Jeremiah 17:7-8, 1 Peter 5:10)

Now to him who is able to do immeasurably more than all we ask or imagine, according to his power that is at work within us, to him be glory in the church and in Christ Jesus throughout all generations, for ever and ever! Amen. (Ephesians 3:20-21)

"You have a God who hears you, the power of love behind you,

the Holy Spirit within you, and all of heaven ahead of you.

If you have the Shepherd, you have grace for every sin, direction for

every turn, a candle for every corner, and an anchor for every storm."

Max Lucado

SEPTEMBER BATTLE PLAN

Focus on Jehovah Raah: The Lord Our Shepherd

"Don't be afraid, little flock, because your Father delights to give you the kingdom".

Luke 12:32

September Agenda

- Fellowship
- Focus on Jehovah Raah: The Lord Is My Shepherd
- Worship
- Requests & Celebrations
- Prayer

Fellowship Starters

The host can ask these questions while mingling or once everyone is seated:

- What is your favorite breakfast food?

- What was your favorite game to play as a child?

Focus on Jehovah Raah: The Lord Our Shepherd

*"The **Lord is my shepherd**; I have what I need. He lets me lie down in green pastures; he leads me beside quiet waters. He renews my life; he leads me along the right paths for his name's sake. Even when I go through the darkest valley, I fear no danger, for you are with me..."* (Psalm 23:1-4)

Jehovah Raah is found in Psalm 23, one of David's most referenced psalms. The Hebrew word ra'ah means *shepherd* and being a shepherd is something David understood personally.

It was a humble and dirty job, reserved for the youngest son of the family. The shepherd was always on duty; all day and all night. Pools of calm water could be difficult to find, predators and thieves were abundant, and the shepherd needed to plant or find sufficient food throughout the year. David's family paid a significant price for their sheep so he took great care in protecting and providing for each one.

He had the heart of a shepherd so he fully understood that he needed a shepherd of his own. He didn't write Psalm 23 from a place of arrogance or self-sufficiency. He wrote in humble recognition of his need for God's provision, protection, guidance, and presence. These are essential truths about God as our Shepherd.

In verse one, David writes, "The Lord is my shepherd; I have what I need." Though our wish lists are often endless, we can always trust God to provide for our needs.

He goes on to say, "he leads me beside quiet waters...he leads me along the right paths for his name's sake." Just as David guided his sheep to pools of still waters and along good paths, the Lord our Shepherd guides us exactly where to walk and when to move (Acts 17:26). We just have to follow his voice.

In addition to providing and guiding, David writes, "You prepare a table before me in the presence of my enemies." (vs. 5) He isn't referring to a dinner table here, but a tableland - the flat top of a mountain or rocky hill, that is covered with grass. It's the perfect place for sheep to graze, but their shepherd must first prepare the land by removing dangerous stones and poisonous weeds, and then keep watch for predators so his sheep can dine in safety. What a beautiful picture of God's protection over us.

Finally, David refers to the comforting presence of a shepherd. "Even though I walk through the darkest valley, I will fear no evil, for you are with me..." (vs. 4) Just as every good shepherd is a constant companion to his sheep, never leaving them to fend for themselves, the Lord our Shepherd is always with us.

When parenting our adult children leaves us at our wits end, not knowing where to turn, the words of Psalm 23 remind us that our children are the sheep of God's pasture. He is their good Shepherd who will go in search of them when they're lost, and pursue them with goodness and faithful love all the days of their lives.

Making it Personal

Which truth about the Lord as my Shepherd brings me the most comfort?

_____

_____

_____

In what ways do I hope that the Lord is shepherding my kids?

_____

_____

_____

A prayer of thanksgiving to my good Shepherd:

_____

_____

_____

_____

_____

_____

Worship Songs about the Lord Our Shepherd:

The following songs may be used to worship God as you prepare your heart to pray. An easy way to find them is to search "Your Soul to Keep Playlist" on Spotify, where the lyrics will scroll for most songs as you listen. If you are going through an especially difficult time, see the "Songs for Extra Hard Days" list on page 301.

- Good Good Father | Chris Tomlin
- He Leadeth Me | Candi Pearson-Shelton
- Highlands (Song Of Ascent) | Hillsong UNITED
- Reckless Love | Cory Asbury

- _____

- _____

September Requests & Celebrations

Use the following pages to record prayer requests and celebrations for each adult child. Remember, no need to fill every box. Simply share as desired.

As you color each space, use it as a guide to direct your prayers.

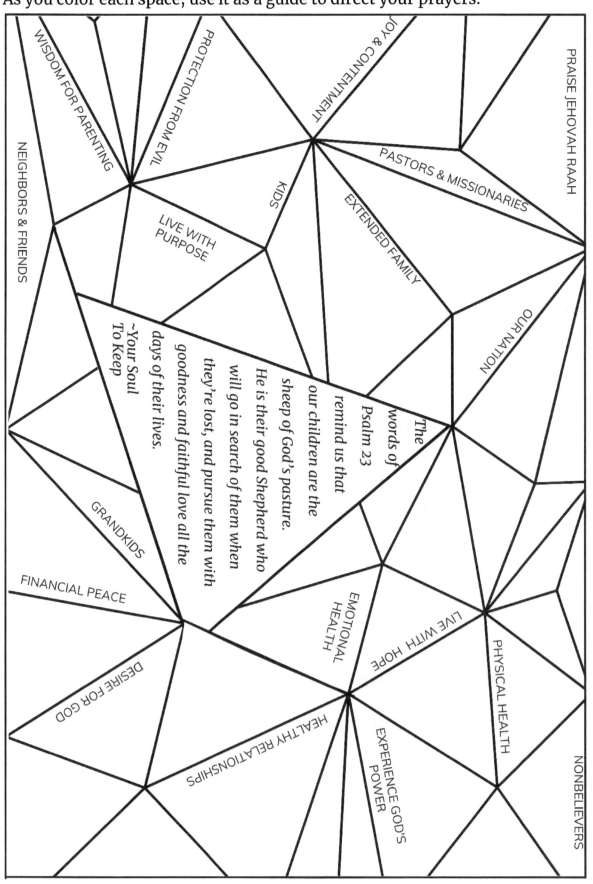

WISDOM FOR PARENTING

PROTECTION FROM EVIL

JOY & CONTENTMENT

PRAISE JEHOVAH RAAH

PASTORS & MISSIONARIES

NEIGHBORS & FRIENDS

KIDS

EXTENDED FAMILY

LIVE WITH PURPOSE

OUR NATION

The words of Psalm 23 remind us that our children are the sheep of God's pasture. He is their good Shepherd who will go in search of them when they're lost, and pursue them with goodness and faithful love all the days of their lives.

~Your Soul To Keep

GRANDKIDS

FINANCIAL PEACE

EMOTIONAL HEALTH

LIVE WITH HOPE

PHYSICAL HEALTH

DESIRE FOR GOD

HEALTHY RELATIONSHIPS

EXPERIENCE GOD'S POWER

NONBELIEVERS

September Requests & Celebrations for: _____

Consider: Celebrations, Mind, Body, Soul, Career & Finances, Family, Relationships

September Requests & Celebrations for: _____

Consider: Celebrations, Mind, Body, Soul, Career & Finances, Family, Relationships

September Requests & Celebrations for: _____

Consider: Celebrations, Mind, Body, Soul, Career & Finances, Family, Relationships

September Requests & Celebrations for: _____

Consider: Celebrations, Mind, Body, Soul, Career & Finances, Family, Relationships

September Requests & Celebrations for: _____

Consider: Celebrations, Mind, Body, Soul, Career & Finances, Family, Relationships

September Requests & Celebrations for: _____

Consider: Celebrations, Mind, Body, Soul, Career & Finances, Family, Relationships

September Requests & Celebrations for: _____

Consider: Celebrations, Mind, Body, Soul, Career & Finances, Family, Relationships

September Requests & Celebrations for: _____

Consider: Celebrations, Mind, Body, Soul, Career & Finances, Family, Relationships

September Requests & Celebrations for: _____

Consider: Celebrations, Mind, Body, Soul, Career & Finances, Family, Relationships

September Requests & Celebrations for: _____

Consider: Celebrations, Mind, Body, Soul, Career & Finances, Family, Relationships

September Requests & Celebrations for: _____

Consider: Celebrations, Mind, Body, Soul, Career & Finances, Family, Relationships

September Requests & Celebrations for: _____

Consider: Celebrations, Mind, Body, Soul, Career & Finances, Family, Relationships

September Requests & Celebrations for: _____

Consider: Celebrations, Mind, Body, Soul, Career & Finances, Family, Relationships

September Requests & Celebrations for: _____

Consider: Celebrations, Mind, Body, Soul, Career & Finances, Family, Relationships

September Requests & Celebrations for: _____

Consider: Celebrations, Mind, Body, Soul, Career & Finances, Family, Relationships

September Requests & Celebrations for: _____

Consider: Celebrations, Mind, Body, Soul, Career & Finances, Family, Relationships

September Requests & Celebrations for: _____

Consider: Celebrations, Mind, Body, Soul, Career & Finances, Family, Relationships

September Requests & Celebrations for: _____

Consider: Celebrations, Mind, Body, Soul, Career & Finances, Family, Relationships

September Requests & Celebrations for: _____

Consider: Celebrations, Mind, Body, Soul, Career & Finances, Family, Relationships

September Requests & Celebrations for: _____

Consider: Celebrations, Mind, Body, Soul, Career & Finances, Family, Relationships

September Prayers

Praising the Lord Our Shepherd

Father, we praise you for being a perfect Shepherd who provides extravagantly, protects fiercely, guides our steps, and never leaves us alone. Your love refreshes our souls and leads us on your perfect path. Even when we walk through dark days, we don't have to be afraid because we are never alone; you are always with us. You wrap us up in your arms, as a shepherd holds his sheep, and comfort us. Your discipline and Truth protect us from wandering away from you. You lift us up in front of our enemies and cause our hearts to overflow with joy. Lord, we pray that your goodness and love will follow us all the days of our lives and that we will dwell with you for all eternity. (Psalm 23)

Desire to Know God

Jesus, your word says that holding tight to your instruction brings life; please cause the hearts of our adult kids to crave your Word. Open their eyes to see that nothing in this life will ever satisfy their desires as fully as having a relationship with you. When the rush of life causes them to feel tired or burned out, we ask that your Spirit will cause them to seek you as a resting place for their souls. When they feel confused, may they never lean on their own knowledge, but be prompted to open the Bible and to search for wisdom and direction from you. And just as the early church found strength in meeting together, we ask that our adult kids would also be drawn to a church family where they will be built up, build up others, and receive the comfort of your Holy Spirit. (Proverbs 4:13, Matthew 11:28-30, Proverbs 3:5-6, Acts 9:31)

Healthy Relationships

Heavenly Father, since the beginning of time you have shown joy and sadness, anger and pleasure. And because our kids are created in your image, they also have strong emotions. Through the wisdom of your Holy Spirit, teach our kids how to use emotion in a wise way so they will enjoy healthy relationships in their marriages, friendships, homes, and with coworkers. We pray they will love others with Godly love, and be guarded against selfish ambition so they will value the interests of others above their own. In marriage, may they fight for one another with one spirit and one mind. And if they ever feel hopeless or helpless, remind them that all things are possible with you. (Genesis 1:27, 1 John 4:7, Philippians 2:1-4, Matthew 19:26)

Experience God's Power

Lord, move in the hearts of our kids so powerfully that their hearts cry out to you, firmly believing that you are the one and only God. When the people of Israel walked away from you to worship other gods, you sent the prophet Elijah to wake them up. But their hearts were hard, so Elijah had two altars built; one for God, one for Baal. "The god who answers by fire; he is God." The people called on Baal from morning until night but no fire came. Elijah drenched his altar with water and called out, "Answer me, Lord, so these people will know that you are God." At once, fire consumed his altar. The people fell on their faces to worship you as the one true God. May your fire consume the hearts of our kids so they will also know for certain that you are God. Crush any rebellion or indecision and powerfully bind their hearts to yours. (1 Kings 18:16–39)

Financial Peace

Lord, make our adult kids as wise as the ants; working hard to provide for themselves and their families even though they have no commander. We believe that you are able to bless our kids abundantly, giving them everything they need to prosper, and we claim that truth right now. We claim that truth on behalf of our kids right now. When they do prosper, guard them against greed and the temptation to seek happiness from material possessions and overwhelm their hearts with the desire to give generously. In marriage, we pray that our kids will have honest lips with regard to their finances; that they will value truth and transparency, and make decisions as a united team. (Proverbs 6:6-8, 2 Corinthians 9:8, Luke 12:15, Proverbs 16:13)

Live with Hope and Purpose

Creator of the universe, you designed each of our adult kids according to your perfect plan; they have a good purpose even when they don't believe it. When your people were thrown out of Jerusalem, they struggled to find hope but Jeremiah told them to build homes, plant gardens, get married, and have babies...to seek peace and prosperity and to never be deceived by false prophets. He reminded them that God was with them - even in exile - and would stay with them until his good promise was fulfilled. When our kids lose their way, we pray that they find new hope and purpose in their wilderness by seeking you with all their hearts. Bring them out of captivity and into the refreshing hope that they are loved...they have purpose...and they are valuable to the God of heaven and earth. (Psalm 139:13-15, Jeremiah 29:1-14)

Wisdom for Parenting

Perfect Father, thank you for our grandchildren and for any who haven't been born yet. Convict our hearts to accept our responsibility as grandparents with sober minds; to obey your command to watch ourselves closely so that we will be Godly examples. We pray that our grandkids will learn to show respect because they witness it in their homes. And we pray they will be kind because kindness is a priority in their home. When our grandkids are disobedient or disrespectful, give their parents the wisdom to set clear boundaries; to let their 'yes be yes' and their 'no be no.' Finally God, we pray that our adult kids will talk about you in their home, when they ride in the car, when they go to bed, and when they get up; so our grandkids will learn to love you, to walk in obedience, and to hold tight to you every day. (Deuteronomy 4:9, Matthew 5:37, Deuteronomy 11:19-22)

Emotional and Physical Health

Jesus, be merciful to our adult kids and flood their minds, bodies, and souls with your living Spirit. Cause them to treat their bodies as living sacrifices; never conforming to anything that will cause physical or emotional harm. May they discern what is good by renewing their minds with scripture and spending time talking with you in prayer, so they will have the grit to persevere when they face hard times. We want so much for our kids to receive the crown of life that you promise to those who love you. Jesus, open their eyes to any pride that is keeping them from experiencing lasting peace and joy, and give us the wisdom to stay out of your way when they are being humbled. Help us to trust that your discipline will lead them to fear you so they will experience abundant life. (Romans 12:1-2, James 1:12, Proverbs 22:4)

Now to him who is able to do immeasurably more than all we ask or imagine, according to his power that is at work within us, to him be glory in the church and in Christ Jesus throughout all generations, for ever and ever! Amen. (Ephesians 3:20-21)

"God sees with utter clarity who we are.

He is undeceived as to our warts and wickedness.

But when God looks at us that is not all He sees.

He also sees who we are intended to be,

who we will one day become."

John Ortberg

OCTOBER BATTLE PLAN

Focus on El Roi: The God Who Sees Me

"Humans do not see what the Lord sees,

for humans see what is visible, but the Lord sees the heart."

1 Samuel 16:7

October Agenda

- Fellowship
- Focus on El Roi: The God Who Sees Me
- Worship
- Requests & Celebrations
- Prayer

Fellowship Starters

The host can ask these questions while mingling or once everyone is seated:

- What high school activities or sports did you participate in?
- What movie do you think everyone should have to watch?

Focus on El Roi: The God Who Sees Me

*"You are **El Roi**. In this place, have I actually seen the one who sees me?"* (Genesis 16:13) Even though these words, spoken by Sarah's servant Hagar, are the only specific reference to El Roi, there are many words in scripture about God seeing us.

"For his eyes watch over a man's ways,
and he observes all his steps. Job 34:21

"...for my gaze takes in all their ways.
They are not concealed from me..." Jeremiah 16:17

"For a man's ways are before the Lord's eyes,
and he considers all his paths." Proverbs 5:21

It's comforting to know that God sees us, isn't it? If he sees us, then he can rescue us from trouble and guide us on the right path. Right?

I mean, when we see a toddler run toward the street, we stop them. When we see a child hurting from the unkind words of a friend, we wrap them up in our arms. When we see our teenager struggling with a decision, we guide them. It's what we do.

And it's what John the Baptist seemed to expect as he sat in prison, hearing about all of the wonderful things Jesus was doing. Striving to be seen, he sent his friends to ask Jesus, "Are you the one who is to come or should we expect someone else?" (Matthew 11:2-3)

Of course, John already knew that Jesus was the one, so it's an odd question. Jesus had seen him from inside the womb, as John leaped inside his mother (Luke 1:41). He saw John baptizing many in the wilderness, even himself (Mark 1:4-9). But John seems to be asking: *Don't you see me sitting here? Can't you see that I need help?*

And Jesus sends a reply that sounds something like this: *Tell John that I am the one who sees the blind and restores sight. I am the one who sees the lame and causes them to walk. I am the one who sees lepers and makes them clean. I am the one who sees the dead and restores life. I am the one who sees the broken and brings good news. And yes, I'm the one who sees John behind bars and leaves him there.*

I'm sure it's not the answer John wanted. But Jesus *did* see John...as a bold prophet, a man willing to die for his belief in the Messiah, and man who would be with him in the kingdom of heaven. Though John could only see his prison cell, El Roi saw the whole picture.

Right now, El Roi sees everything about us, but we only see in part. Right now, we see a dim reflection, but when we are face to face with Jesus, then we will fully know him. Then, we will fully understand. (1 Corinthians 13:9-12)

Making it Personal

What is comforting about knowing that God sees my family?

_____

_____

_____

John could only see his prison walls, but Jesus could see eternity. If I see my own circumstances through an eternal lens, how might they look different?

_____

_____

_____

If I believe that God sees every detail about my adult kids, how might it change how I pray for them?

_____

_____

_____

Worship Songs about the Lord Who Sees Us:

The following songs may be used to worship God as you prepare your heart to pray. An easy way to find them is to search "Your Soul to Keep Playlist" on Spotify, where the lyrics will scroll for most songs as you listen. If you are going through an especially difficult time, see the "Songs for Extra Hard Days" list on page 301.

- His Eye is On the Sparrow | Michael W. Smith
- Psalm 139 (You Are There) | Mercy Me
- Sovereign Over Us | Aaron Keyes
- Watching Over Me | Jason Upton

- _____

- _____

October Requests & Celebrations

Use the following pages to record prayer requests and celebrations for each adult child. Remember, no need to fill every box. Simply share as desired.

As you color each space, use it as a guide to direct your prayers.

DISCERNMENT

EXPERIENCE GOD'S POWER

PROTECTION FROM EVIL

PRAISE EL ROI

EXTENDED FAMILY

WISDOM FOR PARENTING

NONBELIEVERS

JOY & CONTENTMENT

DESIRE FOR GOD

EMOTIONAL HEALTH

I'm sure it's not the answer John wanted. But Jesus did see John...as a bold prophet, a man willing to die for his belief in the Messiah, and man who would be with him in the kingdom of heaven. Though John could only see his prison cell, El Roi saw the whole picture.

-Your Soul To Keep-

LIVE WITH HOPE

KIDS

GRANDKIDS

PASTORS & MISSIONARIES

OUR NATION

FINANCIAL PEACE

PHYSICAL HEALTH

LIVE WITH PURPOSE

HEALTHY RELATIONSHIPS

October Requests & Celebrations for: _____

Consider: Celebrations, Mind, Body, Soul, Career & Finances, Family, Relationships

October Requests & Celebrations for: _____

Consider: Celebrations, Mind, Body, Soul, Career & Finances, Family, Relationships

October Requests & Celebrations for: _____

Consider: Celebrations, Mind, Body, Soul, Career & Finances, Family, Relationships

October Requests & Celebrations for: _____

Consider: Celebrations, Mind, Body, Soul, Career & Finances, Family, Relationships

October Requests & Celebrations for: _____

Consider: Celebrations, Mind, Body, Soul, Career & Finances, Family, Relationships

October Requests & Celebrations for: _____

Consider: Celebrations, Mind, Body, Soul, Career & Finances, Family, Relationships

October Requests & Celebrations for: _____

Consider: Celebrations, Mind, Body, Soul, Career & Finances, Family, Relationships

October Requests & Celebrations for: _____

Consider: Celebrations, Mind, Body, Soul, Career & Finances, Family, Relationships

October Requests & Celebrations for: _____

Consider: Celebrations, Mind, Body, Soul, Career & Finances, Family, Relationships

October Requests & Celebrations for: _____

Consider: Celebrations, Mind, Body, Soul, Career & Finances, Family, Relationships

October Requests & Celebrations for: _____

Consider: Celebrations, Mind, Body, Soul, Career & Finances, Family, Relationships

October Requests & Celebrations for: _____

Consider: Celebrations, Mind, Body, Soul, Career & Finances, Family, Relationships

October Requests & Celebrations for: _____

Consider: Celebrations, Mind, Body, Soul, Career & Finances, Family, Relationships

October Requests & Celebrations for: _____

Consider: Celebrations, Mind, Body, Soul, Career & Finances, Family, Relationships

October Requests & Celebrations for: _____

Consider: Celebrations, Mind, Body, Soul, Career & Finances, Family, Relationships

October Requests & Celebrations for: _____

Consider: Celebrations, Mind, Body, Soul, Career & Finances, Family, Relationships

October Requests & Celebrations for: _____

Consider: Celebrations, Mind, Body, Soul, Career & Finances, Family, Relationships

October Requests & Celebrations for: _____

Consider: Celebrations, Mind, Body, Soul, Career & Finances, Family, Relationships

October Requests & Celebrations for: _____

> Consider: Celebrations, Mind, Body, Soul, Career & Finances, Family, Relationships

October Requests & Celebrations for: _____

> Consider: Celebrations, Mind, Body, Soul, Career & Finances, Family, Relationships

October Prayers

Praising the God Who Sees

Lord, you are the one who sees us; we proclaim your goodness together. Just as you saw the pain of Hagar and the prison cell of John, you see everything about us and everything about our kids. You watch over us as a shepherd watches his sheep, and you see what we cannot see. Teach us to trust you and to believe that you are working all things together for our good. Plant wisdom in the hearts of our kids so they will trust and believe that your ways are better than their own. Thank you for loving us unconditionally and for sending Jesus to forgive our sins. Thank you for grace and abundant life. And thank you for the hope of knowing we will see you clearly someday, when we stand before you face to face. (Genesis 16:13, Matthew 11, 1 John 4:10, Romans 8:28, 1 Corinthians 13:6-12)

Experience God's Power

Jesus, as soon as you told Peter to get out of the boat, he climbed out and walked to you on the water. But when he took his eyes off of you and started looking at the wind and waves, he was defeated by fear and began to sink. Immediately, you reached out your hand and saved him. By your Spirit, call our kids to yourself, just as you called out to Peter, so they will learn to "walk on water." When the wind blows and the waves crash around them, we pray that our kids will keep their eyes focused on you so they won't be defeated by fear or drowned by negativity, sinful desires, or arrogance. When they begin to sink, reach out and save them so they will witness your saving power and praise you. Lord, we want so much for each of them to know you deeply and to walk by faith. (Matthew 14:25–33)

Protection from Evil

Lord, when our adult kids are tempted, open their eyes so they won't be dragged away by unhealthy desires. Your Word says that deception leads to sin and that sin results in emotional, spiritual, and even physical death. Faithful God, protect our adult kids from believing lies that cause them to make reckless decisions and lead to harm. Crush any evil influences in their lives and give them the strength to walk away from unhealthy people and situations. Thank you for the promise that those who dwell in your shelter will be delivered from the snare of the fowler...that those who resist the devil will be rescued from evil. We ask that our kids will have the wisdom to seek you and the courage to flee from the enemy. May your faithfulness be their protective shield. (James 1:13-18, 2 Thessalonians 3:1-3, Psalm 91)

Desire to Know God

Jesus, when you lived on earth you were fully God, yet still desired time with your Heavenly Father. You prayed early in the morning, late at night, alone, with friends, when you were afraid, and when you were dying. No matter what happened in your life, you prioritized time with your Father. Instill the same urgency in the hearts of our kids. May they run to you about every detail of their careers, families, health, and finances, so they will receive wisdom and energy from you. Teach them to withdraw and rest, so they won't be exhausted by the busyness of life. Put people in their path that prompt them to pursue time with you in prayer, in your Word, and at church. When they doubt Truth, invade their minds with your Spirit and make yourself known to them in a way they cannot deny. (Mark 1:35, 1:45, 14:32. Luke 6:12-13, 11:1, 23:46. Matthew 14:23)

Healthy Relationships

Lord, in every relationship - with family, coworkers, and friends - we pray that our kids will experience love that is patient, kind, and supportive; love that shows respect and offers forgiveness; love that isn't easily angered and love that shows compassion. And that they will give this sort of love to others. May they experience relationships that are safe and full of trust, always persevering through difficult times. When others are difficult to love, teach our kids to respond with Godly wisdom. And when the actions or words of our kids cause others to experience pain, open their eyes to what they're doing so they will recognize what needs to change. We pray that they will be quick to say "I'm sorry" and humble enough to seek help. Grow your perfect love in their marriages, Jesus, so that when they are old, they will still be rejoicing together. (1 Corinthians 13:4-7, Proverbs 5:18-19)

Financial Peace

Your Word says that "Those who work their land will have abundant food, but those who chase fantasies have no sense." We pray that our adult kids will work hard every day to provide for themselves and their families, and that their work will be rewarded with profit. Guard them against financial shortcuts that lead to hardship, and give them deep gratitude for all they have so they won't become slaves to greed. By your Spirit, pierce their hearts with compassion so they will recognize the needs of neighbors, coworkers and friends, and be willing to give wise and generous help. When making financial decisions within marriage, we pray that they will always be honest and forthcoming because we know that truth will lead to unity and strength. (Proverbs 12:11, 12:19, 21:5, 22:7. Ecclesiastes 5:10)

Live with Hope and Purpose

Lord our God, we come to you with thankful hearts. Your faithfulness continues through all generations and we pray that faithfulness will be evident in the lives of our adult kids. Protect them from anything we have said or done that is a roadblock to their future wellbeing. By your grace, free them of generational "junk" that robs them of joy or causes them to doubt their purpose. Lord, when our kids pursue new opportunities, direct their steps and keep their ears open to wise counsel. If their plans are in line with yours, then give wings to their dreams so they will experience success. But if they are on a path to disappointment or destruction, then make it clear to them and block their way. When our kids are stubborn, bring humility. When they feel defeated, raise them up to see how beautiful and meaningful life can be when they submit to you as their guide. (Psalm 200:3-5, Proverbs 16:9)

Emotional and Physical Health

Great Physician, we believe you are able to restore emotional and physical health. When our kids are crippled by fear or depression, flood their minds with peace. Your Word says that there is no fear in love, but that perfect love destroys fear. By your Spirit, cause our kids to recognize the enemy's attempts to defeat them, and help them to experience healing by focusing on your eternal plan. If there are physical reasons for emotional struggle, lead them to professionals who can provide appropriate care. Lord, their bodies are your temple, so teach them to make healthy choices. Protect them from harming their bodies with alcohol, drugs, or unhealthy food. As the world bombards them with stress, we claim your promise that they will not be crushed by it. Cause them to put their trust in you so that they will not be destroyed by the chaos of life. (1 John 4:18, 1 Corinthians 3:16-17, Proverbs 17:22, 2 Corinthians 4:7-9)

Now to him who is able to do immeasurably more than all we ask or imagine, according to his power that is at work within us, to him be glory in the church and in Christ Jesus throughout all generations, for ever and ever! Amen. (Ephesians 3:20-21)

"We are not doomed to an ultimate conflict with no hope of resolution. The message of the Scripture is one of victory – full, final and ultimate victory. It is not our doom that is certain, but Satan's. His head has been crushed by the heel of Christ, who is the Alpha and Omega."

R. C. Sproul

NOVEMBER BATTLE PLAN

Focus on Alpha & Omega: The Beginning & the End

"Holy, holy, holy, Lord God,

the Almighty, who was, who is,

and who is to come."

Revelation 4:8

November Agenda

- Fellowship
- Focus on Alpha & Omega: Beginning & the End
- Worship
- Requests & Celebrations
- Prayer

Fellowship Starters

The host can ask these questions while mingling or once everyone is seated:

- What is your favorite thing to do outside?

- Have you ever named your car?

Focus on Alpha & Omega: The Beginning & the End

"'I am the Alpha and the Omega,' says the Lord God, 'the one who is, who was, and who is to come, the Almighty.'" (Revelation 1:8)

Alpha and Omega are the first and last letters of the Greek alphabet, used in scripture to define God as the author of an eternal timeline.

> *He was* the beginning; the Creator of all things. (Genesis 1:1)
>
> *He is* our present help; abiding in us. (Psalm 46:1, 1 Corinthians 3:16)
>
> *He is to come* in the clouds; taking us to his kingdom to reign with him forever and ever. (Revelation 1:7, Daniel 7:18)

Today, we sit on a dot of the eternal timeline; looking back to see years past and forward to events and hopes for the future. But the view from our dot is nothing compared to the view of Alpha & Omega from his eternal throne.

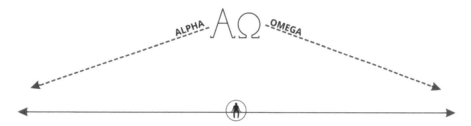

When we try to make sense of our days, with such a limited view, it's so easy to become overwhelmed by fear and anxiety and confusion.

When Joseph's brothers mocked him, threw him in a pit, and then sold him into slavery, he had to be overwhelmed by fear. (Genesis 37:12-28)

When he obeyed God by resisting the sexual advances of his master's wife, but was accused of seduction anyway and imprisoned, he had to feel confused and anxious. (Genesis 39:1-20)

But what Joseph couldn't see was that every tragic event was leading him to a position of great power in Egypt, where he prepared the country for seven years of famine and saved many lives. (Genesis 41:40-54, 41:57)

Alpha & Omega was with Joseph, even when the plan couldn't be seen from his dot on the timeline.

What is the view from your dot today? What is causing confusion or anxiety or fear? Choose to find rest in the truth that Alpha & Omega sees your beginning, your middle, and your end. He is with you now and will be with you tomorrow, and he is working things out in ways you may not see.

"You planned evil against me; God planned it for good
to bring about the present result—the survival of many people."
Genesis 50:20

Making it Personal

How might Alpha & Omega see my current circumstances differently than I do? How might he see the circumstances of my adult kids?

_____

_____

_____

How can an eternal perspective bring me comfort this week?

_____

_____

_____

Write a prayer to God, telling him that you trust him as Alpha & Omega and that you believe he is working things out for good even when you can't see it.

_____

_____

_____

Worship Songs about Our Alpha & Omega:

The following songs may be used to worship God as you prepare your heart to pray. An easy way to find them is to search "Your Soul to Keep Playlist" on Spotify, where the lyrics will scroll for most songs as you listen. If you are going through an especially difficult time, see the "Songs for Extra Hard Days" list on page 301.

- Alpha and Omega | Gaither Vocal Band
- Behold Him | The Worship Project
- How Great Is Our God | Bethany Dillon
- Revelation Song | Kari Jobe

- _____

- _____

November Requests & Celebrations

Use the following pages to record prayer requests and celebrations for each adult child. Remember, no need to fill every box. Simply share as desired.

As you color each space, use it as a guide to direct your prayers.

PHYSICAL HEALTH

HEALTHY RELATIONSHIPS

DESIRE FOR GOD

EXPERIENCE GOD'S POWER

PRAISING THE ALPHA & OMEGA

EMOTIONAL HEALTH

GRANDKIDS

Jesus is our Prince of Peace. His death and resurrection demolish the power of sin and give us the priceless gift of peace that surpasses all human understanding.

-Your Soul To Keep-

GRATITUDE

NON BELIEVERS

LIVE WITH HOPE

WISDOM FOR PARENTING

FINANCIAL PEACE

PROTECTION FROM EVIL

LIVE WITH PURPOSE

OUR NATION

KIDS

November Requests & Celebrations for: _____

Consider: Celebrations, Mind, Body, Soul, Career & Finances, Family, Relationships

November Requests & Celebrations for: _____

Consider: Celebrations, Mind, Body, Soul, Career & Finances, Family, Relationships

November Requests & Celebrations for: _____

Consider: Celebrations, Mind, Body, Soul, Career & Finances, Family, Relationships

November Requests & Celebrations for: _____

Consider: Celebrations, Mind, Body, Soul, Career & Finances, Family, Relationships

November Requests & Celebrations for: _____

Consider: Celebrations, Mind, Body, Soul, Career & Finances, Family, Relationships

November Requests & Celebrations for: _____

Consider: Celebrations, Mind, Body, Soul, Career & Finances, Family, Relationships

November Requests & Celebrations for: _____

Consider: Celebrations, Mind, Body, Soul, Career & Finances, Family, Relationships

November Requests & Celebrations for: _____

Consider: Celebrations, Mind, Body, Soul, Career & Finances, Family, Relationships

November Requests & Celebrations for: _____

Consider: Celebrations, Mind, Body, Soul, Career & Finances, Family, Relationships

November Requests & Celebrations for: _____

Consider: Celebrations, Mind, Body, Soul, Career & Finances, Family, Relationships

November Requests & Celebrations for: _____

Consider: Celebrations, Mind, Body, Soul, Career & Finances, Family, Relationships

November Requests & Celebrations for: _____

Consider: Celebrations, Mind, Body, Soul, Career & Finances, Family, Relationships

November Requests & Celebrations for: _____

Consider: Celebrations, Mind, Body, Soul, Career & Finances, Family, Relationships

November Requests & Celebrations for: _____

Consider: Celebrations, Mind, Body, Soul, Career & Finances, Family, Relationships

November Requests & Celebrations for: _____

Consider: Celebrations, Mind, Body, Soul, Career & Finances, Family, Relationships

November Requests & Celebrations for: _____

Consider: Celebrations, Mind, Body, Soul, Career & Finances, Family, Relationships

November Requests & Celebrations for: _____

Consider: Celebrations, Mind, Body, Soul, Career & Finances, Family, Relationships

November Requests & Celebrations for: _____

Consider: Celebrations, Mind, Body, Soul, Career & Finances, Family, Relationships

November Requests & Celebrations for: _____

Consider: Celebrations, Mind, Body, Soul, Career & Finances, Family, Relationships

November Requests & Celebrations for: _____

Consider: Celebrations, Mind, Body, Soul, Career & Finances, Family, Relationships

November Prayers

Praising Alpha & Omega

Lord, you are the beginning. You created heaven and earth, and every living being. You put stars in the sky and call each one by name. You are Emmanuel; God with us. We don't have to be afraid because you are with us even now. You strengthen us, help us, and hold us in your hand. You rescue us from darkness, transfer us into light, and fill us with fullness of joy. You are the God who is to come. You already know the future and we can trust that your plans are good. One day, Jesus will come back for us, riding on the clouds. Every eye will see him; every heart will know that you are Alpha & Omega. Your home in heaven is perfect and you are preparing a place for us there, so we can live with you forever and ever. (Revelation 1:7-8, Psalm 147:4, Isaiah 41:10, Psalm 16:11, Jeremiah29:11, John 14:2-3)

Experience God's Power

When the Israelites were freed from slavery, they celebrated until the first moment they faced danger and discomfort. Instantly, they were angry and fearful because they assumed you abandoned them, but you never let them out of your sight. You guided them with a cloud by day and a pillar of fire by night. You showed them exactly where to walk and you stood between them and their enemy. They experienced hard, uncertain times but you continued to meet their needs. Our kids live in a privileged country, yet they still get consumed by fears and discomfort. Thank you, Father, for never leaving them alone. Keep their eyes open to your perfect provision so they will see your guidance and feel your presence...even on the most difficult days. (Exodus 13:21-22, 14:19-20)

Protection from Evil

Lord, when our kids think they are walking on the right path, but it is a path that leads to destruction, send an angel to block their way. Just as Jesus prayed for his followers before his arrest, we pray for our children...not that they be taken out of the world, but that you will protect them from evil. When others cause our kids to doubt you, send your Holy Spirit to speak Truth so loudly that they can't deny it. Shield our kids from harm; surround them with a hedge of protection to guard them against every lie that robs them of hope, joy, and purpose. You alone are their protector, and evil cannot dwell near you. Fight for them and be so present in their lives that no evil can stand against them. (Proverbs 14:12, John 17:15, Psalm 5:4)

Desire to Know God

Father, the Bible says that our children will be blessed when they search your Word for wisdom and that it's better for them to find wisdom than money. Set their hearts on fire to learn from you, to spend time with you, and to value time with you above any material thing. May this knowledge guard their lives and lead them on a path to peace. When their eyes are blind to you, send your Spirit to convict their hearts so they will wake up and pay attention to what you say. May Truth be life to their minds and health to their bodies. Grow a desire in our kids to learn from Biblical examples of faith so they will be inspired to throw off sin and get rid of anything keeping them from living an abundant life. May they run with perseverance, with their eyes fixed on Jesus so they will never grow weary or lose heart. (Proverbs 3:13-18, Proverbs 4:20–22, Hebrews 12:1-3)

Financial Peace

Generous Father, we pray our kids will experience peace and joy in their finances; that they will be blessed beyond measure and desire to bless others. Give them the right attitude toward money as you abundantly satisfy their needs, and guard them against caring too much about earthly treasures that quickly fade away. Plant a desire in them to treasure eternal things far more than earthly pleasures. During this Thanksgiving season, prompt our kids to be generous givers; burdening their hearts for those in need so they will experience the blessing of giving with a joyful heart. When our kids have financial needs, put people in their path who will also give generously so our kids will experience your blessing and recognize it as your provision. God, fill their hearts with deep gratitude for every earthly blessing. (Isaiah 58:11, Matthew 6:19-21, 1 Chronicles 29:17-18)

Live with Hope and Purpose

Jesus, lead our kids to spread the joy of the knowledge of you wherever they go. May your light in them bring hope to a broken world. When our kids lose hope, call them out of darkness and into your wonderful light. They are your treasured possession, and you ordained their days before they were even born. Flood their minds with this truth so hard days won't lead to depression. Instead, we pray that they will hear your voice and seek guidance. We rest in the promise that your plans for our kids are good and we surrender to your perfect timing. When answers seem far away, we will trust that you are working in ways we cannot see and thank you in advance for planting hope in their hearts. (2 Corinthians 2:14-15, 1 Peter 2:9, Psalm 139:16-18, Romans 8:18-19, Jeremiah 29:11)

Emotional and Physical Health

Lord, we ask for you to give our kids the emotional and physical strength they need to tackle hard times. When they are weak, may they find strength in you and feel the power of your Spirit filling them with renewed energy. When their bodies are sick or hurt, increase their faith to trust you for healing, just as Jeremiah did when he said, "O Lord, if you heal me, I will be truly healed." In their minds and emotions, teach our kids the secret of being content in every situation; whether healthy or sick, strong or weak. And set them free from any wrong thinking that is causing harm: replace bitterness with grace, self-pity with gratitude, and discouragement with hope. You know their minds intimately and created every cell of their bodies. Take care of them, God. Heal their afflictions so they will rejoice in your provision. (Isaiah 40:29, Jeremiah 17:14, Philippians 4:12-13)

Wisdom for Parenting

Heavenly Father, our grandchildren are like a crown full of jewels. Thank you for the precious ones we already have and for those we've yet to meet. May their homes overflow with stories and songs that celebrate your wonders and power, and may their families embrace the importance of having a church home. When our grandchildren make mistakes, guide their parents to respond with compassion so they will grow up understanding the power of your grace and love. Jesus, in this culture that glorifies rebellion and worships happiness, we pray that our grandchildren will experience Godly discipline, so they will become wise. Fill their homes with the light of your Holy Spirit to guide their parenting decisions, and lead their families on a path to life. (Proverbs 17:6, 14:29, 6:23. Psalm 78:2-4, Hebrews 12:11)

Now to him who is able to do immeasurably more than all we ask or imagine, according to his power that is at work within us, to him be glory in the church and in Christ Jesus throughout all generations, for ever and ever! Amen. (Ephesians 3:20-21)

"Hark! The herald angels sing, 'Glory to the newborn King!

Peace on earth and mercy mild God and sinners reconciled'

Joyful all ye nations rise Join the triumph of the skies

With the angelic host proclaim: 'Christ is born in Bethlehem.'"

Hark! The Herold Angels Sing

DECEMBER BATTLE PLAN

Focus on Jesus: Wonderful Counselor,
Mighty God, Eternal Father, Prince of Peace

"For a child will be born for us,

a son will be given to us...He will be named

Wonderful Counselor, Mighty God,

Eternal Father, Prince of Peace."

Isaiah 9:6

December Agenda

- Fellowship
- Focus on Jesus
- Worship
- Requests & Celebrations
- Prayer

Fellowship Starters

The host can ask these questions while mingling or once everyone is seated:

- What is a home project, craft, or hobby that didn't go so well?

- What is your favorite road trip snack?

Focus on Jesus: Wonderful Counselor, Mighty God, Eternal Father, Prince of Peace

"For a child will be born for us, a son will be given to us, and the government will be on his shoulders. He will be named Wonderful Counselor, Mighty God, Eternal Father, Prince of Peace." Isaiah 9:6

These aren't just names to *call* Jesus. They are reasons to seek him. They are an inventory of the arsenal of wisdom and power available to us through him.

He is our Wonderful Counselor

The actions of Jesus *show* us how to live. The words of Jesus *teach* us how to live. His counsel is supernatural and perfect. Because of him, we have the knowledge of God's mysteries and access to all the treasures of wisdom and knowledge (Colossians 2:2-3). We receive instruction that shows us which way to go, we're surrounded with faithful love, and our hearts are filled with joy (Psalm 32:8-11).

He is our Mighty God

Jesus is the mightiest of warriors; the one who fights for us. He is Master of creation, Ruler of heaven and earth, and Savior of the world. Because of him, we are never alone and we are never defeated. When we pass through rushing waters, we will not be overcome. When we walk through fire, we will not be burned. We are precious to him, created for his glory, and we never need to feel afraid because he is with us (Isaiah 43:2-5).

Jesus is our Eternal Father

A father loves, protects, and sacrifices for his children, but eventually that love comes to an end here on earth. As our Eternal Father, we can trust that the love of Jesus never runs out. He loved us before we were born (Psalm 139:16). He cares for us as shepherds care for sheep; protecting, leading, and providing a satisfied life (John 10:9-10). And he chose to sacrifice himself so that we will not die but have eternal life (John 10:18, John 3:16).

He is our Prince of Peace

Sin destroys peace. It separates us from God, causing emotional pain and spiritual death. But Jesus is our Prince of Peace. His death and resurrection demolish the power of sin and give us the priceless gift of peace that surpasses all human understanding - even in the scariest storms (Philippians 4:7). Because of Jesus, we have power over the enemy and our hearts can overflow with hope (Luke 10:19, Romans 15:13).

Making it Personal

As the parent of adult children, which of these names of Jesus gives me the most hope? Why?

_____

_____

_____

When I am worried because of an adult child, how can I use these names of Jesus to calm my mind and renew my hope?

_____

_____

_____

During the Christmas season, how will I talk to my kids about Jesus and celebrate his attributes?

_____

_____

_____

Worship Songs Jesus

The following songs may be used to worship God as you prepare your heart to pray. An easy way to find them is to search "Your Soul to Keep Playlist" on Spotify, where the lyrics will scroll for most songs as you listen. If you are going through an especially difficult time, see the "Songs for Extra Hard Days" list on page 301.

- Glorify Thy Name | The Worship Initiative
- His Name Shall Be | Matt Redman
- Light of the World | Lauren Daigle
- What a Beautiful Name | Hillsong Worship

- _____

- _____

December Requests & Celebrations

Use the following pages to record prayer requests and celebrations for each adult child. Remember, no need to fill every box. Simply share as desired.

As you color each space, use it as a guide to direct your prayers.

When the waiting gets long and your heart can't make sense of it, trust that El Shaddai knows and that he is working things out in his perfect timing.

– Your Soul To Keep –

December Requests & Celebrations for: _____

December Requests & Celebrations for: _____

December Requests & Celebrations for: _____

Consider: Celebrations, Mind, Body, Soul, Career & Finances, Family, Relationships

December Requests & Celebrations for: _____

Consider: Celebrations, Mind, Body, Soul, Career & Finances, Family, Relationships

December Requests & Celebrations for: _____

Consider: Celebrations, Mind, Body, Soul, Career & Finances, Family, Relationships

December Requests & Celebrations for: _____

Consider: Celebrations, Mind, Body, Soul, Career & Finances, Family, Relationships

December Requests & Celebrations for: _____

Consider: Celebrations, Mind, Body, Soul, Career & Finances, Family, Relationships

December Requests & Celebrations for: _____

Consider: Celebrations, Mind, Body, Soul, Career & Finances, Family, Relationships

December Requests & Celebrations for: _____

Consider: Celebrations, Mind, Body, Soul, Career & Finances, Family, Relationships

December Requests & Celebrations for: _____

Consider: Celebrations, Mind, Body, Soul, Career & Finances, Family, Relationships

December Requests & Celebrations for: _____

Consider: Celebrations, Mind, Body, Soul, Career & Finances, Family, Relationships

December Requests & Celebrations for: _____

Consider: Celebrations, Mind, Body, Soul, Career & Finances, Family, Relationships

December Requests & Celebrations for: _____

Consider: Celebrations, Mind, Body, Soul, Career & Finances, Family, Relationships

December Requests & Celebrations for: _____

Consider: Celebrations, Mind, Body, Soul, Career & Finances, Family, Relationships

December Requests & Celebrations for: _____

Consider: Celebrations, Mind, Body, Soul, Career & Finances, Family, Relationships

December Requests & Celebrations for: _____

Consider: Celebrations, Mind, Body, Soul, Career & Finances, Family, Relationships

December Requests & Celebrations for: _____

Consider: Celebrations, Mind, Body, Soul, Career & Finances, Family, Relationships

December Requests & Celebrations for: _____

Consider: Celebrations, Mind, Body, Soul, Career & Finances, Family, Relationships

December Requests & Celebrations for: _____

Consider: Celebrations, Mind, Body, Soul, Career & Finances, Family, Relationships

December Requests & Celebrations for: _____

Consider: Celebrations, Mind, Body, Soul, Career & Finances, Family, Relationships

December Prayers

Praising Jesus: Wonderful Counselor, Mighty God, Everlasting Father, Prince of Peace

Mary wrapped baby Jesus in cloth and placed him in a manger because there was no room for them anywhere else. As shepherds watched their flocks in the fields nearby, an angel appeared in the light of God's glory to say, "I bring you good news of great joy...Today in the town of David a Savior has been born to you; he is Christ the Lord. You will find a baby wrapped in cloth and lying in a manger." Lord, thank you for sending your son and for the wise counsel, protection, peace, and eternal life available to us because of Jesus. Make us bold to proclaim this truth to our adult kids this Christmas, and fill us with wisdom as we embrace life with the beautiful truth that our Savior is also our Shepherd; guiding us, protecting us, and giving us abundant life. (Isaiah 9:2-7, Luke 2:7-14, John 10:7-11)

Experience God's Power

Father, send clarity and guidance into the lives of our adult kids. When Mary became pregnant, you told her exactly what was happening and what to do. When Jesus was born, you told the shepherds exactly what was happening in Bethlehem and showed them exactly where to go. You replaced fear with joy and they found Jesus...just as you said. Countless people in the Bible found hope and joy because they listened to your truth and followed your guidance. May the same be true for our kids. As they listen to Truth, give them power to overcome fear and step out in faith. As they follow your voice, guide them. And as they recognize your power in their lives, may they feel blessed. Even as I speak these words, send your power of clarity and guidance. (Luke 2:8-20)

Protection from Evil

Jesus, may our kids be strong because of your mighty power. Their struggles aren't against flesh and blood, but against the powers of this dark world so teach them to put on your armor so they can stand against the devil's schemes. Send your Spirit to teach them how to stand firm, guarded with Truth and righteousness. May they be ready to share your gospel and to use your shield to stop the flaming arrows of evil. Protect them with your helmet of salvation and sword of the Spirit. May they crave your Word and fight with spiritual weapons that demolish any strongholds keeping them from experiencing abundant life. You say that we will have trouble in the world but that you have overcome the world. Thank you for this promise; may it be evident in the lives of our adult kids. (Ephesians 6:10-17, 2 Corinthians 10:4)

Desire to Know God

This Christmas, make the joy of your salvation real to our kids in a new way. Bring revelation that causes them to seek Jesus, and send your Spirit to speak Truth that causes them to receive your gift of grace. For our kids who know you but are distracted by the details of life, bring them fully back to you with undivided hearts. Remind them that you are the vine and they are the branches; apart from you they are nothing. Renew their desire to live their faith with actions that bring glory to you. For our kids who actively seek you, bless them in a special way this Christmas and reward their obedience. May all our kids delight in your Word, becoming like well-watered trees that yield fruit in season and whose leaves never wither; whatever they do will prosper as they draw near to you. (Psalm 1:1-3, John 15:4-5)

Healthy Relationships

Father, send your Holy Spirit ahead of our family this Christmas, so each of us will have patience and grace for one another. May we love in humility, being quick to forgive, just as you forgive us. May our conversations honor you and build each other up. For our kids who feel lonely during this season, encourage their hearts and fill any void in their life with your sufficiency. For our kids who are in relationships, guide them in wisdom so they will have one mind and one spirit as they face decisions about gifts and social commitments. In their workplaces, help our kids to be a blessing to coworkers and bosses. May their contributions be recognized, mistakes quickly forgiven, and their actions be an example of your love and grace. (Colossians 3:13, Ephesians 4:3-4 and 29)

Financial Peace

Lord, as our kids make financial decisions about the holidays, give them wisdom to sit down and count the cost so they will shop wisely and not put themselves in a financial bind. Convict them to be honest, so money never causes a lack of trust in their relationships, and guard them against seeking joy and satisfaction in material things. We pray that they will desire to bless those in need so they will store up treasures in heaven. Lord, where our kids are working hard to provide for themselves, we thank you and ask that their work ethic be rewarded with recognition and profit. When they are discouraged about work, cause them to stay diligent until another path becomes clear. We pray that our kids will be content in every circumstance; whether well-fed or hungry, living in plenty or in want. Teach them the secret of being content so they will experience financial peace. (Luke 14:28-30, Proverbs 12:22, 1 Timothy 6:17-19, Proverbs 14:23, Philippians 4:11-12)

Wisdom for Parenting

Thank you, Jesus, for the grandchildren we already have and for any that may come in the future. More than anything, we pray that the homes of our grandchildren will overflow with stories about you so they will be rooted and built up, strengthened in faith and overflowing with gratitude. Throughout the holiday season, give our adult kids wisdom in their parenting choices. May they be models of your love and grace, and talk about the true meaning of Christmas. Guard them against becoming too busy so they will spend quality time with each other, instilling your values in the hearts of our grandkids. Jesus, go before them and prepare their hearts to find joy in family gatherings and to focus on being a blessing to one another, so that whether they eat or drink or whatever they do, they will do it all for your glory. In this way, our grandchildren will experience peace, kindness, and unconditional love. (Colossians 2:6-7, Corinthians 10:31)

Emotional and Physical Health

God, you are an ever-present help in trouble and we pray that our kids will seek you whenever they feel afraid or worried. Though the earth gives way and the mountains fall, you are their Almighty Lord and you are with them. Teach them that the Spirit that raised Jesus from the dead is also available to them. In every storm, may this truth help them to be still and know that you are God. When they experience physical pain or illness, we claim the power of your Spirit to heal them. When they are harmed by unhealthy habits, open their eyes to it and cause them to seek you for the strength to make changes. We lay them before you and claim the promise that you have not given our kids a spirit of fear, but of power, love, and sound judgment. Free them from wrong thinking and bind their minds to yours, so they will walk in light. (Psalm 46, Romans 8:11, 2 Timothy 1:6-7, John 8:12)

Now to him who is able to do immeasurably more than all we ask or imagine, according to his power that is at work within us, to him be glory in the church and in Christ Jesus throughout all generations, for ever and ever! Amen. (Ephesians 3:20-21)

RESOURCES

"For Christ also suffered for sins

once for all, the righteous for the unrighteous,

that he might bring you to God."

1 Peter 3:18

God's Gift of Salvation

If I stood before God right now and he asked why he should let me into heaven, what would I say?

Would you tell him you go to church? That you're a good person? Would you think that a loving God should never ask such a question? Maybe you would just stand there in silence, not knowing what to say.

Truth is, **nobody** is *good enough* to make it to heaven. Nobody.

The Bible says that all of us sin and that the cost of our sin is spiritual death - eternal separation from God and the abundant life he offers (Romans 3:23). It also says that salvation can't be earned by any good work we do (Ephesians 2:8-9).

So then, what's the answer? We stand on the edge of a chasm with death on one side and life on the other...unable to cross.

But that doesn't have to be where it ends. God loves us desperately; so much that he chose to make a way for us to cross that chasm.

"For God loved the world in this way:
He gave his one and only Son,
so that everyone who believes in him
will not perish but have eternal life." John 3:16

Because of the death and resurrection of Jesus, we have hope. Because of him, we can be forgiven and cross the chasm: The Bible says, "*If you confess with your mouth, "Jesus is Lord," and believe in your heart that God raised him from the dead, you will be saved. One **believes** with the heart, resulting in righteousness, and one **confesses** with the mouth, resulting in salvation.* Romans 10:9-10

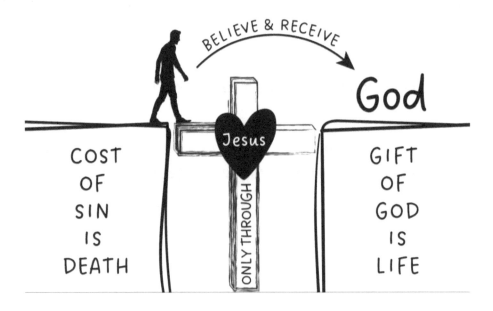

Are you ready to tell God that you believe that Jesus died on the cross and rose again, to pay the price of your sin? Are you ready to receive his gift of salvation? The following words don't save you, but if they represent the cry of your heart, then God will hear them and you will be saved.

> *Dear Jesus, I know that I've sinned and I'm sorry. I believe that you died on the cross and rose again so that I can be forgiven and spend eternity in heaven with you. I also believe that you have a good purpose for my life and that you will teach me how to live. Thank you for loving me. Amen*

Welcome to God's family!

The Bible says that angels rejoice when even one person repents, so smile big knowing that heaven is excited to have you in the family! (Luke 15:10) Becoming a Christian doesn't fix your current problems or protect you from future ones, but it means that you will never again face any problem alone. You will never again have to wonder if there is a purpose in them. His purpose is to produce perseverance in you and to fill you with lasting joy, no matter what life throws your way.

As you dance into your new identity as a child of God, there are a few things to hold close to your heart. First, God's Spirit is alive in you and he will never leave you. Second, the Word of God (the Bible) is an important tool for learning more about him and how to make wise choices. Finally, encouragement is found in spending time with other people who love Jesus. So, how does all of this work? Here are a few tips to get you started:

Talk to Him

A healthy relationship requires communication, and your relationship with God is no different. Talk to him in prayer about *everything*; what you're worried about, what you **need**, and what you're thankful for. When you take everything to him in prayer, he promises to fill you with peace that passes understanding and to guard your heart and mind. (Philippians 4:6-7)

Learn from Him

Reading the Bible is an important way to build your relationship with God. If you don't have one, check out biblegateway.com or the YouVersion App. Both have many suggested reading plans, but it's always good to start simply by reading the book of John. As you read, ask God's Spirit to teach your heart to be strong and wise. Another great way to connect with God daily is by reading *Our Daily Bread*, a free resource available at _www.odb.org_. We like to keep a copy on the powder room counter, because...well...you know.

Grow with Others

First, find someone to tell about the decision you made to receive God's gift of salvation so they can celebrate with you. If you're not sure who to tell, tell me: KristiDusenbery@TheLaughingGrandma.com. I'd love to hear your story!

Next, connect with a local church that teaches from the Word of God. Just as receiving God's gift of forgiveness seals your eternal fate, spending time at church and with others who love Jesus will impact the quality of your life here on earth.

If you need help finding a church, visit *www.churchfinder.com* to browse websites that tell what different churches believe, how they grow relationships among Christians, and how they tell others about God's gift of salvation.

Song Index

January: Our God Who Provides

- Blessed Be Your Name | Matt Redman
- Good, Good Father | Chris Tomlin
- Goodness of God | Bethel Music, Jenn Johnson
- Great Are You Lord | Casting Crowns

February: The Lord with Us

- Another in the Fire (acoustic) | Hillsong UNITED
- Holy Spirit | Francesca Battistelli
- I Am Not Alone | Kari Jobe
- Never Once | Matt Redman
- There Was Jesus | Zach Williams, Dolly Parton

March: The Lord Who Heals

- Come Alive (Dry Bones) | Lauren Daigle
- Healer | Casting Crowns
- Healer | Bethel Music, Leah Mari
- The Hurt and the Healer | Mercy Me
- There is Power | Lincoln Brewster

April: The Lord Who Sanctifies

- Amazing Grace (My Chains Are Gone) | Chris Tomlin
- Cross Medley | Anthem Lights
- The Old Rugged Cross | Chris Rice
- Living Hope | Phil Wickham

May: Our God Almighty

- El Shaddai | Amy Grant
- Good God Almighty | Crowder
- Holy Holy Holy | Hillsong UNITED
- Salt & Light | Lauren Daigle

June: The God Who Gives Victory

- God, I Look to You | Bethel Music
- Surrounded (Fight My Battles) | Bethel Music, Kari Jobe
- The Lion and the Lamb | Big Daddy Weave
- Way Maker | Leeland

July: The Lord of Peace

- God of Peace (acoustic) | Eagle Brook Music
- It Is Well With My Soul | Joey + Rory
- Leaning On the Everlasting Arms | Selah
- Tremble | Mosaic MSC

August: The Lord of Armies

- I Will Fear No More | The Afters
- Lift My Eyes | Alisa Turner
- Mighty to Save |Hillsong Worship
- Whom Shall I Fear (Angel Armies) | Chris Tomlin

September: The Lord Our Shepherd

- Good Good Father | Chris Tomlin
- He Leadeth Me | Candi Pearson-Shelton
- Highlands (Song Of Ascent) | Hillsong UNITED
- Reckless Love | Cory Asbury

October: The Lord Who Sees

- His Eye is On the Sparrow | Michael W. Smith
- Psalm 139 (You Are There) | Mercy Me
- Sovereign Over Us | Aaron Keyes
- Watching Over Me | Jason Upton

November: Alpha & Omega

- Alpha and Omega | Gaither Vocal Band
- Behold Him | The Worship Project
- How Great Is Our God | Bethany Dillon
- Revelation Song | Kari Jobe

December: Jesus

- Glorify Thy Name | The Worship Initiative
- His Name Shall Be | Matt Redman
- Light of the World | Lauren Daigle
- What a Beautiful Name | Hillsong Worship

Songs for Extra Hard Days

- Because He Lives | Gaither Vocal Band
- Blessings | Laura Story
- Come As You Are | Crowder
- Give Me Jesus | Fernando Ortega
- Into the Sea (It's Gonna Be Okay) | Tasha Layton
- It Is Well | Bethel Music
- Just Be Held |Casting Crowns
- Lift My Eyes | I Am They
- Press On | Saleh
- Thy Will | Hillary Scott
- Trust in You | Lauren Daigle

THE
LAUGHING
GRANDMA

TheLaughingGrandma.com
Prov. 31:25

About the Author

Life is definitely a journey and here is a tiny bit about mine.

My husband Tim and I were married just days after my twentieth birthday. Less than a year later, his job moved us from Des Moines to Omaha and I put my college career on hold. Might as well start a family, right? We were young, had no savings and plenty of debt, and we were *so* unprepared. Still, I wouldn't change a single thing. God has faithfully used every struggle to shape us and grow us up.

Thanks to the financial and emotional support of our parents, and our commitment to each other, we were able to battle through some pretty rough days and turn our "vintage" mobile home (with orange shag carpet and no air conditioning) into a place we loved. By the time we celebrated our sixth anniversary, we had welcomed three baby boys and I was thoroughly enjoying mom-life.

At forty years old, I finally earned the teaching degree I began pursuing so many years earlier, followed by my master's degree in 2015, and today I am an elementary instructional coach with an amazing staff of dedicated teachers. Public education is a gut-wrenching, exhausting endeavor. Please remember to pray for the many public-school teachers who go to work every day, filled with the desire to make a positive impact in their own little corner of this crazy world.

So, about those three baby boys; they grew up, joined the Air Force, married amazing women, and blessed us with six precious grandbabies. Today, they are settled into civilian life and doing a fabulous job of keeping our prayer lists full. The grandma years are packed full of chaos, love, tears, valleys and laughter...the perfect reason to passionately pursue Jesus every day.

Inspired by my family and the crazy world we live in, I created *The Laughing Grandma* blog and Facebook page, with the hope of inspiring parents and grandparents to shine the joy of Jesus into the lives of their families, and to *laugh without fear of the future*. (Proverbs 31:25)

**To learn more, stop by TheLaughingGrandma.com
and follow @thelaughinggma on Facebook.**

THE
LAUGHING
GRANDMA

TheLaughingGrandma.com
Prov. 31:25

Also Available from Kristi

The 'Before'
Books & Coloring Books

Before We Open Presents

The perfect way to kick off your Christmas celebration. The book tells the beautiful truth that YOU are the reason Jesus was born in the first place. Young kids will enjoy finding God's bright star on each page and the whole family will receive a personal reminder that they are deeply loved by God. The companion coloring book reinforces the message of the book with illustrations and Bible verses to color and activities to help them understand how much God loves them.

Before We Hunt for Eggs

A colorful way to kick off your Easter celebration. Whether it's the gold egg that reminds us of heaven or the red egg that reminds us of the blood on the cross, every page tells a truth about the true meaning of Easter. Young kids will enjoy searching for the bunny and the whole family will be reminded that they are designed for a beautiful purpose. The companion coloring book reinforces the message of the book with illustrations and Bible verses to color and activities that focus on God's beautiful plan of salvation.

Baby showers? Birthdays? Grandkids? Neighbors and friends? Sunday school kiddos? Give them the gift of these ten-minute traditions with eternal impact.

Stop by TheLaughingGrandma.com to learn more.

References

Arthur, K. (2000). *Lord, I want to know you: A devotional study of the names of god.* WaterBrook Press.

Batterson, **Mark**. *Praying Circles around Your Children.* Zondervan, 2012.

Boom, Corrie Ten, et al. *The Hiding Place.* Chosen Books, 2006.

Cummings, **W. H.** (Arranger). (1855). Hark! The Herald Angels Sing [Adapted from Felix Mendelssohn's "Festgesang"].

Elliott, C. (1835). Just as I Am [Hymn].

Graham, B., **Toney**, D., Graham, F., & Graham, B. (2011). *Works., Billy Graham in quotes.* Thomas Nelson.

Lawrence. (2008). *The spiritual maxims of brother Lawrence.* Wilder.

Lewis, C.S. *Mere Christianity*: Harper One, 2015

Lucado, M. (2001). *Traveling light: Releasing the burdens you were never intended to bear.* W Pub. **Group.**

MacArthur, **John**. *Ephesians: Our Immeasurable Blessings in Christ.* Thomas Nelson, 2016.

Omartian, **Stormie**. *Prayer Warrior: The Power of Praying Your Way to Victory.* Harvest House Publishers, 2013.

Ortberg, **John**. *Love Beyond Reason: Moving God's Love from Your Head to Your Heart.* Zondervan, 2001.

Sproul, R. C. (2023, July 24). *R.C. Sproul: Satan does not hold the keys of death.* ChurchLeaders. https://churchleaders.com/pastors/455171-r-c-sproul-satan-does-not-hold-the-keys-of-death.html

Spurgeon, Charles. *The Treasury of David.* Marshall Bros., 1881.

Spurgeon, Charles. In *Spurgeon's expository encyclopedia: Sermons / volume 11*. Baker Book House, 1988.

Thornton, **Corallie**. *Watch out! Godly Women on the Loose.* Ark House Press, 2009.

Made in United States
Troutdale, OR
01/08/2024